To Kevin –
It's Great to
You with us. Go
You & keep up the
work.
6-21-02

SOME SAW MUD, I SAW STARS

by

BERNADINO PAVONÉ

with Lowell Cauffiel

Peacock Press
38777 W. Six Mile Road
Suite 300
Livonia, Michigan 48152-2692

Manufactured in the United States of America

ISBN 0-9721001-0-5

For George Safie and Lila Joseph

1958 – 1976

*

They were young and in love,
dying together in a tragic accident
and leaving a hole in my heart
and a void in my life.

PUBLISHER'S NOTE

Some Saw Mud, I Saw Stars is an autobiography based on recollections, official records, and conversations and interviews with key participants. Several individuals, in consideration of their privacy, have been assigned pseudonyms. Their names appear in italics in the first reference.

ACKNOWLEDGMENTS

It's been said: "A man wrapped up in himself is a small package."

Indeed, this book — the personal and financial success detailed here — remains linked to the influence and work of others who've impacted me in so many ways.

My wife, Lisa; mother, Gloria; sister, Theresa; and father, Bernie, with his wife, Helen, lead the list for my gratitude. Lisa for her love; Mom for her drive and focus; Dad for his principles and steady direction; Helen for accepting me like a son; and Theresa for her care and inspiration.

My entire family was a treasure chest of support, including all those who made the years glorious at "The Big House" — a family home — next to Safie Drive. I also have to thank my godparents, Uncle George and Aunt Madeline Safie for their continuing guidance; Uncle Charles Safie for his business teachings; Aunt Joanne for her loving heart; and my Uncle Pat Pavoné for his example of character. I need to thank cousins, Charlie Rashid, Enzo Pavoné and Steve and John Safie, for their camaraderie and good cheer. The younger generation in my family inspires me also, including my cousin, Salvatore, 14. I have tried to help him as a mentor and have reaped much satisfaction from the experience. His parents, Rita and Joe LaTorre, have been an inspiration to me, always treating me with respect. Many other family members who appear in this book have played a big part in my life.

In my book, ICR co-founder Abood Samaan is considered a family member, as well as my great friend. So is Jerry O'Connor, as his wisdom and straight talk have been fatherly throughout the many years of our friendship.

I also want to thank my wife's parents, Ron and Sokum Amatangelo, for accepting me into their family, and my brother-in-law, Nick Amatangelo, for joining us at ICR. My sister's husband, Tony Borrello, I love as a brother.

As for this book itself, much of the material here would not have been possible without Warren and Kitty Jameson, who did the initial interviewing for this project.

My gratitude and thanks also go to:

— Detroit District Judge Wade McCree, who has helped me on various fronts, including his professional counsel and his friendship. I am deeply indebted to him;

— Todd Renzi, a very bright and insightful executive who was instrumental in developing our computer software, the key to ICR's success;

— Masters Sam Santilli and William Adams, who not only taught me karate but discipline and respect for others;

— Attorney Christopher Andreoff, who handled my criminal case and was a constant source of support;
— Judge Herman Campbell, of Shelby Township's (Michigan) 41st District, for his friendship and support;
— John Graves, Ph.D., who never lost faith and introduced us to the higher education market;
— Robert Kelly and Stuart Logan, two talented attorneys from the Dykema Gossett law firm. They have been invaluable in their counsel to me;
— Jerry Benefield, former president and CEO of Nissan, for his business advice and friendship;
— Danny O'Connor, who works for ICR and whose talents in photography helped in this project;
— Fr. George Charnley, of St. John Neumann parish, for his friendship, counsel and invaluable spiritual guidance;
— Lowell Cauffiel, a wonderful and talented writer, whose skills with words helped me tell this story.

Of course, I want to express my gratitude to the ICR sales representatives and employees for their loyalty, dedication and hard work. They have helped make ICR the success it is. Their focus on our vision and opportunities are the ingredients of which happy endings are made.

CHAPTER 1

JUNE 29, 1994

We left Michigan in the morning, following I-75 through Ohio, then across Kentucky's rolling bluegrass counties where horses grazed behind the whitewashed fences of thoroughbred estates. South of Richmond, the Daniel Boone National Forest greeted us with the western ridges of the Appalachian Mountains. As we swerved and dipped through the spectacular scenery, the family Oldsmobile should have been filled with conversation.

Instead, we were numb.

My mother, sister and I had said few words during the 432 miles from Detroit. What could be said? Waiting at our destination in Manchester, Kentucky was my future — a future with very limited opportunity. Manchester had a population of only 1,800 people, and surrounding Clay County, not even 25,000. But I would not be given the chance to meet even a half dozen folks at the local country store. The town's largest employer was an electrical manufacturer with 400 workers. My business was with Clay County's second largest employer, the Federal Correctional Institution.

Everyone called it FCI Manchester.

It is a federal prison.

Two miles outside the town limits, we turned into the parking lot. There were two facilities — one a minimum security camp with two buildings and dormitory style rooms, no fences, and the 500 inmates enjoyed freedom of movement around the grounds. The other was the medium security prison, featuring an administration center and four austere housing units in grey concrete. Its inmate population was some 1,000 federal felons. Built in 1992, the grounds of the complex were immaculate. Manchester's medium high-security facility could have easily been mistaken for a small community college had it not been for the double fences and razor wire.

As we walked into the administration building I was certain I was prepared. I carried a piece of Louis Vuitton luggage, its contents still fresh with the scent of a fine department store. I'd packed new designer pajamas, a new Fila jogging suit, a new $150 pair of Nike running shoes, new Calvin Klein underwear and new Calvin Klein socks. I was going to make myself as comfortable as possible. I was simply checking into a hotel, I'd told myself.

The clean lobby only reinforced that delusion.

"My name is Bernadino Pavoné," I told the receptionist sitting at a desk in the administration building. "You're expecting me. I guess I'm what you call a self-surrender."

Seconds later, two guards came out — a man and a woman. The male guard eyed my luggage.

"You're not going to need that," he said.

Suddenly, the bag was gone.

No, I tried to explain, I'm designated to go into the minimum security camp. That's where they sent white collar criminals, not the prison itself which handled higher-risk inmates serving up to 35 years.

"I'm a self-surrender," I repeated.

"No, Pavoné, you're designated to be behind the fence," the male guard said.

I turned to my mother and sister. Tears were streaming down their cheeks. I come from a family steeped in Mediterranean traditions. Family is close. Family is most important. I was suffering, and so were they. When one family member suffers, the entire family does. The female guard watched us embracing and her eyes welled up, too.

"I love you. I'm so sorry, mama mia," I said.

And then they were gone.

Seconds later, I stepped through a sliding glass doorway. It closed behind me and another door opened just ahead — it was the gateway into the prison. I saw keys in the hands of the two guards. As we moved deeper into the facility they opened another door, locking it behind me before they opened another door just ahead.

This is not a hotel, I thought.

"This is receiving," somebody said.

"Take off your clothes," said a guard.

A strip search began.

"Do you have any drugs?" the guard asked.

"No."

"Do you do drugs?"

"No, I do not."

The female guard who watched the farewell to my family seemed concerned. She began talking, saying the scene in the lobby was a sad one.

"I don't know why you're here," she said.

I told her I'd pled guilty to breaking a federal law. I was a convicted counterfeiter.

"Well, you don't belong here," she said.

I looked her in the eyes.

"No, I *do* belong here," I said.

They gave me a khaki shirt and a matching pair of pants. There would be no comfortable running sneakers. They gave me prison shoes, supplied by the federal government — black shoes with black laces with black rubber soles. The shoes felt tight and stiff.

They took my picture and minutes later handed me a stark, stunned image of myself on a prison ID card. Underneath it was my federal prisoner number and my birth date. The month before, I'd turned 29.

They explained the rules as we walked to one of the housing units. Everything seemed to happen quickly, but also very methodically. More doors unlocked, then locked. I stopped and waited. Then, only when told, I moved. I walked down hallways of unpainted grey cement block, my stiff shoes squeaking on the well-waxed floor. From one window I saw the yard and the glint of razor wire. It looked sharp and hot in the southern Kentucky sun.

This is hell, I decided. The prison was clean and orderly, but I'm in hell. I couldn't shake that thought.

They locked me in a cell that contained a dozen other prisoners. There were several rows of double bunks. I glanced at the faces of my cellmates, then set a blanket and other items I'd been issued on a lower bunk.

No, take an upper bunk, somebody said. Lower bunks were a privilege. New prisoners had no stature here.

Only time could give me that.

That night, on an upper bunk, I lay on a thin mattress, listening to the distinctive sounds found only in a prison. Hushed voices, then a shout of profanity. Doors opening and closing. Gate motors groaning. Latches slamming shut.

Then, “Lights out!”

The certainty of where I was, and where I would remain for two years, seeped into my consciousness.

Then the pain began, a piercing just under my rib cage. It grew into a deep ache. I pulled my knees up to my chest. It was a kind of emotional pain I’ve never known before, and one I’ve never known since. I kept seeing my mother and sister in the lobby. I kept thinking about all those who knew I was here.

I asked myself: What have I done? How could I do this to my family? How could I hurt my loved ones so much? And one more question — the most important one:

What can I possibly do to set this right?

Seven years later, I would be able to answer those questions. I could answer them because, as I lay on the bunk, I had embraced one positive thought: In two years I’d be going home. I’d made a mess of my life, but it was not beyond repair. Serving time was a beginning, not an ending. Prison, in its own way, was a second chance.

All I had to do was take it.

After my release, my stature was not defined by a prison pecking order. In 1994, a Detroit federal judge sentenced me to two years in prison. Seven years after prison, I’m blessed with the trust of thousands of company executives, representatives and customers. In 1994, I’d let my family down. Seven years later, many family members worked with me and shared in my success. In 1994, I was known as federal prisoner No. 16184-039, but in 2001 as co-founder, president and CEO of ICR Services, Inc., I operated what *Inc* magazine called in that year one of fastest-growing, privately held companies in America.

The lesson of FCI Manchester remains with me. Every day presents a new beginning, not only for me, but for those who are joining our company's ranks. My story is not unlike the challenges being met by thousands of others who've come into ICR Services and found success after what appeared to be a personal dead end.

In 2002, ICR Services, and all its assets, were valued at approximately $400 million, and the company was free of debt. A business that began with the simple goal of repairing credit for Americans, is international with representatives in the U.S., Canada and Puerto Rico. It has four divisions: ICR Financial, ICR Communications, ICR Health and Wellness and ICR Automotive Technologies. The parent company, with the four divisions, offers 16 different products and services. In 2002, we had 50,000 company sales representatives, but our growth potential is virtually unlimited and immune from stock market fluctuations and economic downturns. And we're doing it not with empty promises or puff and stuff. We're doing it by helping people and keeping our word.

How did this all happen? How did I hit bottom, reach a turning point and rise to heights I couldn't even imagine that sleepless night in a prison bunk? It is a journey populated with many good people — and some not so good. But it is my story. I take responsibility for my choices, for my failures. Both the failures and successes have made me what I am today.

It's a story that begins with family. It's a story that begins two generations before I was born.

CHAPTER 2

FAMILY FOUNDATIONS

My grandfather experienced firsthand how wages, credit and debt could shape a life, a family, a future.

After emigrating from the northern Italy province of Calabria, Joseph Pavoné worked in the coal mines and coke yards of Orient, Pennsylvania. In lieu of pay, the company gave workers credits they could only spend at the company store. Prices were arbitrarily determined by the coal company, often at great profit, so the workers were constantly in debt. With a family of eleven children, survival was more than difficult. My father, Bernard J. Pavoné, Sr., often told me a story about the winter the credit ran out.

"My father had to make a trip to the Salvation Army in Uniontown," he'd recall. "I'll never forget my brother Pat and I huddling together, waiting for Dad to get off the cable car with food. I will always be grateful to the Salvation Army for helping us out. But I told myself when I got older, I'd do anything — dig ditches, anything — rather than work in that coke yard and live like that."

At 19, my father left Pennsylvania and came to the Detroit area, taking a job at a dollar an hour repairing sewing machines and working in shipping and receiving in a small textile company. He became an apprentice tool-and-die maker in the auto industry. Prior to graduation from his apprenticeship, he enlisted in the U.S. Air Force to fulfill his military obligation. While in the service he bought my grandfather a house with 10 lots in Pennsylvania. He ultimately retired as an executive from the Ford Motor Company.

The Safies, my mother's ancestors, also came from the kind of family that was not afraid to travel great distances to find a better life. My maternal grandfather, Dimitri Safie emigrated from Damascus, Syria as a young man, joining his brother, Khalil, to start a small produce farm in New Baltimore northeast of Detroit. Grandpa married a Syrian, and my mother was the youngest of their eight children.

A little ingenuity launched the Safie family business. My grandfather and Great Uncle Khalil often would grow more peppers than they could sell at market. So the family canned the surplus vegetables. My mother recalls washing peppers in the bathtub. The canned products became so popular that farming became secondary to the operation. They built a cannery on the New Baltimore property and the Safie Pickle Company was born.

My mother was 23 years old when she met my father while bowling one night on Detroit's east side. My dad, then 27, was working for Ford. My sister, Theresa, was the first child from their marriage, and two years later I came along and, apparently, I was a handful as soon as I could stand.

"Bernie became a crib jumper overnight," my dad liked to tell people. "He had this trick where he'd jump higher and higher until he'd flip over the railing. Then he'd yell for help as he hung desperately from the rail."

I've heard other stories. Apparently I had an insatiable curiosity during the terrible twos. My mother banned me from the kitchen because I was incessantly exploring cupboards and cookware. She said she had to hold my hand everywhere we went because I would bolt from her side and go exploring. Once, I'm told, I caused quite a fuss at a major Detroit department store. My mother was standing with me next to a clothes rack when a manager came up.

"Do you know that your son stopped the escalator?" he asked.

"How do you stop an escalator?" she asked.

"Why don't you ask him?"

I'd apparently discovered an emergency stop button while she'd been shopping.

Mischief forms my earliest memories. I was a willful child when it came to school and play. I wanted things done my way and could convince other kids to follow. I remember always getting in trouble for talking too much in church nursery school. The scoldings had little effect and I remember being kicked out of the school at five.

"Think about it," my mother would say later. "How many children do you know who were kicked out of kindergarten for talking too much?"

Theresa looked after me in school, often steering me away from trouble. She was the ideal student — courteous, charming and frequently won awards for scholastic achievement. Of course, I tried to ride on the coattails of her good name. The teachers had a hard time believing we came from the same parents. Yet, my grades also were pretty good, and I loved to read. By the end of the third grade, I was reading at the level of a high school freshman with 90 percent comprehension.

While I often tested the rules at school, I attempted only one major rebellion at home. It came a few months after my fifth birthday. I was mad at Mom for reasons that I can't even recall. The short of it was: I decided to run away.

She told me, "If you're running away, you better pack all your clothes. And don't worry about coming back."

I put some things in a little backpack and headed downstairs where my father was waiting.

"What do you think you're doing?" he asked.

"I'm running away. Mom said I can."

"Okay," he said. "But first, let me give you something before you go."

He picked up a Converse high-top tennis shoe. The next thing I knew it was smacking across my backside. That hurt. I cried, but he did, too. When he let go, I went upstairs to my room and cried myself to sleep. It was the only spanking I ever received from Dad, and that was the end of my plans to run away.

In the ensuing years, there never was a reason to leave. Our suburban house in Mt. Clemens, 30 miles northeast of Detroit, had one of the few built-in pools in the neighborhood. It was a popular place to hang out with cousins and friends. My mother was very accepting of everyone who would gravitate to the pool in the summer.

More importantly, love and attention filled the home. My mother saw us off to school and was waiting for us when we returned. Dinner time was family time and we always ate together. Mom grew up with Syrian cuisine, and still enjoys cooking Syrian food. We savored her mouthwatering dishes and were encouraged to talk about our day. Dinner fostered communication and camaraderie. In today's economy, with both parents working in many cases, family dinner time can be hard to arrange. That's a great loss. For me, family traditions established the kind of trust and security that eventually would carry me through more difficult days ahead.

My father and mother had very different personalities.

Integrity and responsibility dictated my father's view of life. You told the truth and kept your promises, he'd say. These were traditional Italian values. He was the second oldest in his family, and before moving to Michigan, was the oldest boy in the household after his older brother left to join the Navy. After seeing how his father's lack of education kept him in the coke yards, he embraced continual self-improvement in his adult life. He was always going to school, earning associate degrees and certificates that helped him move up the ladder at Ford.

"Keep applying yourself," he would always say. "Your education never stops."

My mother, however, took a more unconventional approach to life. Some of her brothers and sisters had traditional Syrian marriages. She not only didn't have an arranged marriage, she married outside her culture. In general, she accepted little at face value and encouraged a healthy skepticism.

Syrians are often great negotiators, a practice learned at the public marketplaces of the Mideast. My mother was never hesitant to question a product, a service, a price. If you were not happy with a service, you let someone know. It was okay to ask for a manager. It was okay to seek a lower price and Mom always got her deal.

My mother also had an entrepreneurial spirit, cultivated no doubt by her family's success in the pickle business. She encouraged us to try whatever we wanted to do. My mother stressed that it was the individual that made things happen. It was not education or the company or the boss that was going to carry you, it was *you*. *You* had to overcome the obstacles and the odds and the naysayers.

You had to find people who shared your vision. *You* had to find a way to make it happen. Your destiny was in your hands.

Both parents, however, were united in one message: Honesty and keeping your promises were not negotiable.

I tested that once at the age of seven and I still remember the results. There was a Seven-Eleven store not far from the house where I'd go to buy treats. One day I stole a piece of bubble gum and that night I couldn't sleep because I felt guilty. So I woke up my parents in the middle of the night and confessed.

They took the penny theft very seriously. There was a long talk in my room. The upshot was I had to go back and tell the woman who worked behind the counter what I had done.

The next day I went to the store and confessed. To my amazement, the woman behind the counter, who was the owner, gave me a Slurpie.

"Whenever you come in here, I'm going to have a Slurpie waiting for you," she said. "I'll never forget your honesty and the courage it took to tell me."

Integrity. Work ethic. Education. Finding your own dream. And the importance of family. These were the messages delivered in the house in Mt. Clemens. They'd produced a good life for a coal miner's son from Pennsylvania and opened up new horizons for the youngest daughter of Syrian immigrants. They are great values.

Looking back on the early years, I realize I had one more advantage. Not 15 minutes from my home was a special place where I could watch my parents' ideals come into play.

CHAPTER 3

THE BIG HOUSE

We called it "The Big House" — a two-story, red-brick, Cape Cod with green and white awnings and cavernous rooms with nine-foot ceilings. It seemed smaller to me when I visited as an adult. But it remains larger than life in the memories I gathered as a child.

If ICR Services, which I would develop years later, has a beginning, it was at the Big House where it had its birth.

The house was owned by my uncle and godfather, George Safie, my mother's brother, who lived there with his wife, my Aunt Madeline, and their five children. It was located in New Baltimore, just around the corner from Safie Drive. Many relatives lived on Safie Drive: Aunt Joanne, Uncle Charlie, Uncle Louie, Aunt Theresa, Uncle Tom and Aunt Eleanor Deeby and their kids. The Safies also owned nearly 800 acres of bordering land which once served as my grandfather's farm. (Given the dominance of the Safies in the neighborhood, Uncle George convinced authorities to name the street after the family.) Weekends in my grade school years were spent at the Big House and at other family households on Safie Drive. If we visited one house, we had to visit the others in the neighborhood so no one was offended. Hospitality was a family tradition. Sometimes that meant eating several meals a day at several different houses. Tabbouleh, hummus, Syrian bread, fruit, bulgar, and rice pudding filled the tables.

For me, the visits meant hanging out with my cousins. There were a dozen other boys my age to play with and plenty of property for our gallivanting horde to roam. We played hide-and-seek and kick-the-can. We measured and chalked a football field behind Uncle Tom and Aunt Eleanor's home. We played baseball on a diamond behind my Uncle Charlie and Aunt Joanne's home. We played until we were exhausted. Then we'd go inside to eat and play backgammon and other board games. Between the boys and all my female cousins, we were noisier than a dozen jackhammers. None of the adults seemed to mind. They were too busy tweaking up the volume in their own animated conversation and uproarious laughter.

The Big House was headquarters, not only because of its size, but because it was located adjacent to the Safie Pickle Company, the combination packing plant and warehouse owned by my uncles. It was an 82,000-square-foot building in white cement block that my young eyes perceived as endlessly spacious and long.

My mother often talked about the company's history. When her father first came from Syria, he planted peppers in the fields behind the Big House. At harvest time, the family packed the peppers in bushel baskets and took them to Detroit's Eastern Market, 30 miles away, arriving two hours before dawn.

"Whatever they didn't sell, they brought back to a little garage where they had installed a bathtub," she told me. "They'd wash the peppers and place them in jars in a brine of vinegar, salt, and water to preserve them. At first, they gave the jars away. Then they packaged and sold them to stores."

As my uncles took over the business, they developed the capacity to process and package pickles. But the demand for peppers was greater than what they could grow. So they let their land lie fallow and began buying produce from other farmers. Eventually, the factory was automated so they could process and package 32 kinds of pickles. My family expanded into production and labeling for Vlassic, Kraft, and Aunt Jane's brands in addition to their own line.

Pickles are a seasonal business, with the fresh-pack season running from June through October as the produce ripens in the fields. During these months, some 300 employees worked in two shifts in the Safie Pickle Company. They bottled, packaged and distributed pickles, peppers and other products. The company shipped all sizes — pints, quarts, gallons, and 50-gallon barrels. After the fresh-pack season, produce would be shipped in from warmer climates, and a smaller workforce ran the plant. But during the peak season, the entire extended family went to work. That included my 38 cousins and friends we would recruit. The pace was frenetic, the hours long. But because so many family members were involved, we also had a lot of fun. We joked with one another, played practical jokes and rarely took orders or criticism personally. We all had a common goal: Get the product to market, and everyone could share in the success.

The factory was my introduction to the world of business. I was intrigued by systems and procedures used by the company. Behind the factory were several 20,000-gallon vats for processing pickles and peppers. When ready for packaging, the produce was transferred to smaller vats inside the building. From there it was graded, sliced and prepared for the automated bottling lines.

In full production, several bottling lines churned away at once. So it was noisy. Over all that racket, the front office often paged people over the P.A. system. Managers and mechanics scrambled up and down the floor to troubleshoot production problems and broken equipment. It might have seemed like chaos to an outsider, but I felt an overwhelming sense that everything and everyone was working together — a harmonic synergy I could sense even as a young boy. I loved the intensity of the Safie Pickle Company.

My mother often told the story about the day the cannery came to a sudden halt. In the office there was an emergency safety switch which could stop all the automated processing lines. One day, when she was a teenager, a mouse darted across the office floor. My mother screamed and my Uncle Charlie threw the safety switch, shutting the entire plant down. After my Uncle George rescued her from the top of a desk, it took a couple hours to get the plant moving again. Thousands of dollars in productivity were lost. I always thought it was curious how something as seemingly insignificant as a mouse could set into motion a series of events that would impact an entire facility.

I had an insatiable curiosity for detail and how things got done. My Uncle Charlie and Aunt Joanne used to walk my cousin Stevie and me down grocery aisles and I would check for family products in area stores. No matter where we went, we'd find Safie pickles. Uncle Charlie explained step by step how products reached the consumer. I learned about marketing, pricing and building customer loyalty. Sometimes, I'd see a customer reach for the family brand in the store. That always gave me a thrill. I saw a successful enterprise at work — and my family owned it.

Before I ever reached middle school, I already was getting ideas.

I spent a lot of time with my cousin, Stevie, who was my age. We built forts together, rode bikes and threw eggs at cars. But between our mischief, we found ourselves talking business. We wanted to build a company like our family had. Later, in our early teens, we opened a produce stand. We'd go to Detroit's Eastern Market with Uncle George, negotiate a good price from farmers and bring the fruits and vegetables back to New Baltimore and sell them by the roadside. Looking back at it now, I can see how Stevie and I were captivated by qualities that elude many businesses today. The Big House, Safie Drive and the pickle company represented the idea that you *can* mix work and play. In fact, they augment each other. Add to that a family approach to the enterprise — that you don't just make money for yourself, you share your success with those you work with every day.

I remember a serious conversation Stevie and I had one afternoon.

"When I do something, I want you to be working with me," I told him.

"And the same for me," he said. "We'll be partners when we grow up."

We pinkie-swore it. We were only eight years old.

That's how my mind was already working in the third grade.

CHAPTER 4

FRACTURED DREAMS

The year was 1976. America celebrated its bicentennial. Businesses were discovering the facsimile machine. The French introduced Perrier water to an increasing market of health-conscious Americans. And a movie called "Rocky" set box office records with a story about overcoming the odds, not only for its lead character, but for Sylvester Stallone who wrote the script and cast himself in the title role to rescue his fledgling acting career.

It was the year my world began falling apart.

My mother and father never argued. Theresa and I never saw a cross word between them. In fact, I didn't see my father as much as I would have liked because of his evening school schedule. He gave his love by providing for the household. That was his way. But as a child, I wanted a role model for daily problems, so I often turned to older cousins, aunts and uncles on the Safie side to fulfill my needs.

Dad was a quiet man with an unshakable demeanor. At first that provided a nice balance for my energetic mom, but apparently not for the long haul. As she got older, she wanted to explore business opportunities. She wanted to travel — travel abroad in search of adventure.

"We simply grew apart," she later told me.

The fact we'd not seen a cross word between them perhaps made it more traumatic when my sister and I were told we'd be moving in with my Uncle George and Aunt Madeline in the Big House. Talk of divorce was in the air. My parents didn't want us witnessing the rancor during this difficult time. I was 11 years old and confused by the sudden turn of events.

However, I was thankful for the Big House where I was loved and accepted like a son. I was with family. They helped me remain in my original school district in Mt. Clemens. My cousins, Theresa, or Mary drove me to grade school every morning in rush hour, stopping first for breakfast at Big Boy. I was so happy I didn't have to transfer schools I made Theresa a promise. She was always talking about Jaguars, her favorite car.

"I'm going to buy you a Jaguar," I told her.

"Right, Bernie," Theresa would say. "In your dreams."

Dreams were getting a little harder to come by, but not all was lost. In the Big House I roomed with my older cousin, Georgie, who was 18 years old, and my cousin, Johnny, 15. I was an adolescent and I couldn't have been with better male role models.

Georgie was perfect — everything I wanted to be when I became his age. He was handsome, athletic and always on the move. I can still picture him running into the pickle factory with some important job to do, often with a sandwich in his hand. He was always hungry. He'd eat a box of cereal and drink a gallon of milk for breakfast out of a big green Tupperware bowl, but had the thin, chiseled body of a wide receiver. Georgie, at one time, was voted "King" of L'Anse Creuse High School.

He was that popular. His girlfriend, Lila Joseph, was the pageant queen of Mt. Clemens. She was intelligent, vibrant and a beautiful woman of 18.

At night, we filled his bedroom with music and conversation. Georgie loved the Beatles. Soon I'd memorized every song of his favorite album at the time, "The Magical Mystery Tour." With the Beatles as a backdrop, we'd talk about cars and motorcycles and girls. Some of my cousins were taking karate lessons. I told Georgie I was thinking about trying the martial arts, but I knew my parents had to resolve their problems first. We talked about my parents and my future. Georgie was gentle and a good listener. He was there for me, and I leaned on him for support.

One time I told them, "Hey, Georgie and Johnny, I'd like to take you to show and tell."

"Show and tell what?" they asked.

"You know, take you to my class. Show them how cool you are."

They laughed, but I was serious. I felt that way not only about Georgie and Johnny, but about other cousins such as Stevie and Charlie Rashid. Even with my parents' marriage on the rocks, I had something special with my extended family. The Big House was my emotional safety net.

But soon even that would change.

Six months into my stay at the Big House, big plans were underway for Christmas. Many of the Safies were planning to head to the Safie house in Florida for the holiday.

A few days before we were set to leave, I rode with cousin Georgie to a local Firestone dealership. Georgie's Ford Thunderbird was in good shape, we thought, but in need of new tires. We watched the mechanic raise the car on the hoist and examine the underside with a shop lamp.

The mechanic walked over. "Forget the tires for now," he said. "You have a more serious problem."

"The car's got lots of problems," Georgie said.

The mechanic shook his head. "Well, this one's dangerous. Your trunk is rusted out. You can get exhaust inside the car. Carbon monoxide, and you know what that can do."

We walked over to the car. I remember staring up at the hoist, looking at the jagged hole in the underside. Georgie looked up, too, shrugging his shoulders.

"Hey, that's no big deal," he said. "That's been there for awhile."

The mechanic wiped his hands on a shop rag. "Myself," he said,"I'd take care of it ASAP. In fact, I'd rather walk than ride in that car."

But Georgie, I'm sure, wanted to hang onto his money for the holiday trip. "I'll fix it as soon as I get back from Florida," he said.

The mechanic lowered the car, and we drove away.

The night before the trip, everyone was excited. Most of my aunts and uncles were heading to the Sunshine State as well. That meant more than two dozen cousins on the loose in the tropics. It was December 16, nine days before Christmas. Georgie drove off that night to see his girlfriend, Lila. He wanted to say goodbye.

The next day, my mother picked up my sister and me from school. She told me I needed a haircut, so we went to the family's favorite barbershop, Phil's Barber, a busy operation with a dozen chairs. Everyone there knew the family. Normally, the barbers would joke and kid with me. Instead, everyone was silent. When I looked at people, they looked away.

I didn't know that horrible news had already spread throughout the town. I didn't know that only an hour earlier my mother had been at the county morgue identifying my cousin's body.

We stopped at the house in Mt. Clemens where she broke the news to me slowly, one step at a time, the way police officers are trained to do.

"There's been a bad accident with Georgie," she said.

"What kind of accident?" I asked. "What do you mean?"

She said Georgie and Lila had been found in his car, parked near 24 Mile Road. "It would probably be better if Georgie passed away because his brain is dead and he can't move at all," she continued. "It would be a blessing, in fact."

"What happened?" I demanded.

She said Georgie and Lila had been asphyxiated by carbon monoxide fumes. They were making out in the backseat and had apparently fallen asleep, I later found out.

"I'm sorry, honey," she said. "But Georgie died. He didn't make it."

"You're lying," I said. It was the only time in my life I've ever accused my mother of dishonesty.

"No, Bernie."

"He can't die. He's too young."

I don't remember clearly what happened next. But my mother says I threw myself on the ground. I kept screaming that she was lying.

Later that afternoon I was forced to confront the truth. When we arrived in New Baltimore to join the Safie family, television trucks were parked in front of the Big House. Inside on the family TV, the tragedy was already being reported on the evening news. The Big House was filled with relatives as it so often was on the weekends. But this time, people gathered quietly in small groups. I remember walking among them, looking at their faces. I remember everyone's stunned eyes.

The funeral procession was more than five miles long. The Joseph family was as large as ours. The town of New Baltimore was in shock. Georgie and Lila were two popular teenagers with bright futures. Many in the community joined the families to pay their last respects. Georgie and Lila were buried in graves side by side.

I will never forget the strength of my mother. I never saw her cry through it all. She appeared to hold the entire Safie family together, attending to the details others were too grief-stricken to handle. She counseled her siblings and her nieces and nephews. After the services, she took Aunt Madeline, Georgie's mother, to the cemetery every day for two weeks. I saw what today I consider "character" — the ability to serve others in times of great hardship and heartache.

But for me, Bernie Pavoné, the family I so cherished had suffered a major loss. I had suffered a major loss. My hero had fallen because of a moment of procrastination over a 12-inch hole in the trunk of his car. Like the mouse in the cannery, everything had changed because of one seemingly small detail.

It was a family crisis even more frightening than my parent's pending divorce. And little did I know it was only one in a series of calamities yet to come.

CHAPTER 5

STEPFATHER FROM HELL

Not a year after my cousin's tragic death, a new set of circumstances unfolded, all of them carrying with them other forms of trauma and loss.

Shortly after my parent's divorce, my mother married a man who'd swept her off her feet. My stepfather, *Dr. Rene,* was a respected surgeon and successful urologist. We moved to his house in Plymouth, a western Detroit suburb, far from the eastern suburbs and the Big House I knew so well. Many Detroiters perceive Woodward Avenue, which divides the east and west side of the city, as a border of sorts. Many families don't venture to the opposite side of town; they risk getting lost when they do.

For my sister, Theresa, and I, moving to Plymouth was like landing on the other side of the world. I was 12 and facing all the ramifications of puberty, not to mention the uncertainties of a new school, a new neighborhood and new friends.

Those would be the least of my worries, I'd soon learn.

First, no one could ever replace my dad. Any child who's ever had divorced parents understands the loss and confusion of only seeing a father on weekends. Within that context, any stepfather's role is a difficult one, too.

If there was anyone up to the challenge, my stepfather appeared to be the man. He made my mother very happy during their courtship. He was more than an ample household provider, earning about $750,000 a year. It was more money than I could even imagine at my age. I remember thinking: how in the world can someone make that much money? I couldn't imagine what he did at his office and the hospital every day. My mother, Theresa and I would never want for anything. We'd moved into a beautiful Spanish-style villa in a pristine neighborhood. The good doctor was generous not only with his new family, but with his patients. He was one of the few physicians who would still make house calls for patients too ill to come to his office. If someone couldn't afford to pay, he'd rip up the bill. But the urologist had a secret, one we all learned in the weeks just after the marriage vows were exchanged.

I remember the first incident. It started with the muffled sound of yelling coming down the hall to my new bedroom. Theresa and I ran to investigate. Our stepfather was in a rage, yelling at my mother, throwing household items around the living room. I'd never heard our father raise his voice to my mother. I'd never heard a man call my mother the names my stepfather was screaming that night.

Theresa and I retreated to her bedroom. Both of us were scared to death. Our stepfather stood a good six feet, his overweight frame only adding to his suddenly intimidating presence. I felt helpless, powerless to do anything. And I was confused. What had turned "a very nice man" into a raving lunatic? My sister and I seemingly had come face to face with a real-life Dr. Jekyll and Mr. Hyde.

The first New Year's Eve in our new home began to provide the answer. The house was filled with guests and my mother was the consummate hostess for a gathering of her new husband's friends. Theresa and I milled around the party, anticipating the celebration as the clock ticked from 1977 to 1978.

Instead, we watched our new stepfather turn into a pig. It's the only way I can describe it. As the night wore on, the well-spoken physician transformed into a swaggering, foul-mouthed party killer. He was rude to his guests. He insulted my mother. Yet, he seemed completely oblivious to the embarrassing impact he was having on the event. The whole time he had a drink in his hand, consuming copious amounts of liquor.

The good doctor was a drunk, an alcoholic.

The signs became more evident in the weeks and months ahead. The doctor would rise at the predawn and head into the hospital for a day of surgery and office appointments, then return home at 7 p.m. and head directly to his vodka. He'd drink it on the rocks with Fresca. He'd keep drinking through the entire evening. The longer he drank, the more his personality transformed into a surly, thin-skinned tyrant, quick to criticize or demean anyone who he imagined a threat to his boozy space. He had astonishing capacity, often consuming a fifth in a single sitting. He also had an amazing ability to recover, always waking up early and heading off to work. His colleagues later told me his hands were always steady and his mind clear during surgery. Then after a day of practicing medicine, he'd return home to the bottle and start the entire cycle all over again.

Alcoholism, I've since learned, affects one in four American households. Only a small percentage of those afflicted with the disease ever seek help, and of those who do, only two out of ten realize long-term recovery. Often, recovery is initiated by a life changing experience, or "hitting bottom," as they say in Alcoholics Anonymous. Many alcoholics have to lose everything before they're ready to attend AA meetings and make the difficult changes in their thinking and living habits to stay away from the first drink.

My stepfather would not be one of the fortunate ones. He would always cite his own professional success as a physician to convince himself he didn't have a problem. But his personal life, his family life, was an ongoing disaster.

I clearly remember where the good doctor would often end up late at night. The basement of the home was beautifully finished. My stepfather had a handsomely decorated home office, a Spanish-style iron gate serving as the doorway. Sometimes, I'd see him in the room in the early morning hours, just sitting with a bottle in arm's reach. Sometimes he'd be passed out, his face flat on the desk. It was a striking image through those iron bars. He may have been a brilliant doctor with a six-figure income, but he was in his own prison.

And we all became his fellow inmates. It's an established family dynamic associated with alcoholism: Those who love or live with an alcoholic are thrust into a world of chaos, confusion and broken promises. They begin to walk on egg shells and bury their emotions in an attempt to keep the drinker from becoming worse. Their own thinking becomes distorted. The disease impacts their lives even though they don't drink.

As a young teenager, of course, I knew little of these concepts. I just knew that in the seven years my mother was married to this man, I lived with a bully. I was his number one target. He put me down incessantly, belittling my hobbies, my schoolwork and my choice of friends. He was insanely jealous of the attention my mother showed my sister and me. He pouted if she wasn't attentive to his every need.

When he and I were alone, it often was worse. He called me foul names and flicked cigarette butts at me.

"You little bastard," he'd snipe.

A well of anger filled to the brim as the months and years dragged on. I found ways to drain it, gravitating toward aggressive pursuits and sports. I got a drum set and took lessons. I felt a certain relief wailing on those drums in the basement, and a certain satisfaction knowing the noise was no doubt getting under my stepfather's skin.

In our first year at the new house my mother bought me a Yamaha YZ-80 motorcycle. I took several spills, but always remounted.

Soon, I discovered acres of raw, hilly land around Plymouth — terrain perfect for bike jumping. I'd gun my bike just before hitting a little rise, and fly through the air. I crashed a few times, but wasn't deterred. Soon, I was jumping farther than any of my friends. I broke my hand one day in a head-on collision with another rider. But I couldn't wait to get the cast off to get back on my machine. Maybe I couldn't do anything about a stepfather who beat me down, but I could damn sure conquer those hills.

My mother and sister took different tracks to keep their sanity. Mom was convinced she could somehow help her new husband. She was not the kind of person to give up on something or someone easily. A family friend, Jerry O'Connor, helped her to understand the disease. A recovering alcoholic, Jerry had logged more than 20 years of sobriety in Alcoholics Anonymous. My mother steered my stepfather to AA meetings. But every time he went, he'd return and promptly get smashed.

My sister detached, pouring her efforts into school and work. She later told a friend: "I neither liked nor trusted my stepfather. He wanted to pay my way through school and buy my first car, but I accepted nothing from him. Mostly, he ignored me and focused his anger on Bernie. Maybe my femininity protected me. Knowing he was an alcoholic, I avoided the man, but he went after Bernie."

He tormented all of us. I was afraid for everyone. One winter night, he grabbed a knife and chased my sister and me around the house in the snow. We were in our underwear. It was a bad scene, one of many. I couldn't sleep many nights because I was scared that my stepfather would beat my mother. He never actually beat her, but a couple of times he pushed and shoved her. Once he threw a statuette at her, striking her foot. We had to take Mom to the hospital for stitches.

That night, I confronted him.

"She is my mother," I said. "Don't you *ever* do anything like that again, or I'll kill you."

I glared at him, but I was terrified. I stood hardly five feet. He could have taken me out with one swipe of his hand.

I talked to my mother alone later. "Mom, I promise I'm going to get you out of this," I said. "One day your life is going to be a dream."

How I was going to do that seemed elusive, maybe even impossible at the age of 13. But soon I found myself thinking about my cousins on Safie Drive and the sport some of them pursued. A few classmates in my Plymouth school were also getting into it. They were training in town.

I researched the details with a friend who was enrolled. I enlisted his father into the effort to sell my mother on the sport.

"Let him," he told her. "The sport will give your son self-discipline."

It was karate, but I had something other than "sport" in mind.

CHAPTER 6

BULLY PATROL

If my classmates were being picked on, I rushed to their rescue. If a smaller student was being left out and not getting his turn with the ball, I took it from the big guy and gave it to the little guy. This tendency to help others dated back to early grade school. Where it came from is anybody's guess. It's simply my nature to help people who had the odds stacked against them.

The impulse fostered its share of problems. Often I wasn't directly in trouble, but always seemed to be around it. That meant trips to the principal's office and phone calls home to my mother. I came to the aid of small kids being picked on during recess. I jumped on boys who made fun of retarded kids. When a group of new students transferred to my grade school after their school shut down, they tried to take over our playground, I stood up to them. Racism, too, carried me into conflict, not only on behalf of minority students, but myself. My black hair and olive skin from my Mediterranean heritage inspired ethnic slurs. I answered the insults directed at me or my family with my fists.

For some reason, I was fearless about getting hurt in the fights that ensued. I was relentless in battle. That state of mind usually carried me to victory, no matter what my opponent's size.

"Bernie had lots of fights at school," my mother told a friend once. "But he never came home beat up."

With the ongoing verbal abuse from my stepfather at home, I took to the martial arts like a gladiator who had been granted the opportunity to fight his way to freedom. I began with basic lessons in 1978 and eventually moved on to a powerful style of karate developed in Okinawa called Isshin-ryu. Five days a week, I trained an hour in the morning before school in preparation for a grand national tournament. Then I returned to the "dojo," or karate school, two times a week for evening classes. I dropped out of high school sports to focus on the martial arts. Four years after I started training, I was Grand National Champion and successfully defended my title in 1983.

Sam Santilli, my master, became a major influence in my life. Outside the protocol of the dojo, many of his students dropped the traditional instructor title of "Sensei." We called him "sir."

Santilli infused discipline into us. It was not an easy place to earn your black belt. Details were all important. You stood at attention and if your belt wasn't tied correctly, or you weren't presenting yourself properly, you were reprimanded. It was, "Yes, sir," or "No, ma'am." "Yeah" or "nah" were unacceptable. The karate was full contact. If you broke a nose, you stayed and finished the bout.

Discipline. Attention to detail. Persistence. That was my master's way.

Santilli also regularly addressed the proper use of the powerful skills we were learning. You acted as a gentleman and did not pick fights. You pursued dialogue with an aggressor and tried to reason. But if someone threatened you, you had every right in the world to defend yourself. Your boundary was a three-foot circle around you, or the length of your kick. If someone crossed that line, they were in a position to hit you or stab you or inflict bodily harm. When that line was crossed the talking stopped. They had entered your strike zone. At that point, without further warning, you took them out.

A turbine of anger revolved in the center of my boundary zone, driven by my stepfather. Seeing the affect of his tantrums on my mother made me furious. Home life was like living with one of those "On the Air" signs that dictate silence in TV studios. We had to be quiet at breakfast when he was hung-over. When he left, everyone would sigh with relief. When he returned home, the silence light lit again. Mom always had dinner waiting and the house was spotless. She tried hard not to give him anything to criticize, but he still found plenty to bitch about once the booze took hold. I would lay awake nights, the adrenaline rushing through my body. I wanted to lay him out, but he was off limits.

After all, he was my mother's husband.

My school work suffered. I found it hard to focus on subjects. During classes, I took on teachers intellectually. My mother had always taught me to question things, to apply curiosity and logic if I wasn't satisfied with the answers. But often I took it to extremes. I found myself on a mission. I could do nothing about the injustice at home, but that didn't mean I couldn't take on the world at-large.

I rode the bus with a boy named Arnie who had severe learning disabilities. My first day with him I watched people pick on him. He just sat there with the usual vacuous smile. When someone twisted his ear, I saw the hurt in his eyes.

I put out the word. Nobody picks on Arnie, and nobody did.

One day, school officials eliminated the bus stop where Arnie and I had been getting off for a short walk to his house. I always walked with Arnie or he'd wander down the center of the street, and when a car came along, he didn't know what to do. When they eliminated the stop, I decided that was too far for him to walk, given the physical problems he also had. When the bus neared Arnie's home the next day, I talked to the driver.

"Let us off here," I said. "It's too far for Arnie to walk from the next stop."

"This ain't no taxi," she said.

"All right," I said. "Then when you get to the next stop sign, we're getting out."

When the bus reached the intersection, she rolled through it. It was her way of refusing my request. I pulled out my notebook, noted the time, date, and location. I wrote across the top of the page, "I saw the bus driver, Mrs. Hall, run a stop sign at Concord Drive and Beacon Hill at the time given above." I convinced all 15 student passengers to sign it.

The next morning I was called out of class and ordered to the office of the area coordinator, the school district's administrator for student problems. Mom and the bus driver were waiting outside the office. My mother and I went in.

"What's the problem, Bernie?" the coordinator asked. "You're on the swim team, you play football. Surely you can walk a couple of extra blocks so we don't have to contend with all this fuss."

"It isn't me," I said. "It's Arnie." I explained the situation and added, "When I get back on the bus again, I'll do the same thing."

Mom laid into me for talking back to adults. But when the bus driver was brought in, Mom laid into her too. Before the meeting was over, the bus stop was returned to its original location.

I found other causes, or they found me. I looked after another student in a wheelchair so no one would bully him. I didn't go with anyone to my seventh-grade dance, but spent the night dancing with an overweight girl who looked forlorn in the corner. She'd been a frequent target of school tormentors. I interjected myself into a lot of situations where bullies normally went unchallenged. In fact, I hunted for them. I never started an altercation, but I defended the underdog.

These days, educators and social workers are addressing the school issue of peer harassment. But back then, teachers often handled such matters off the record. Twice teachers in middle school enlisted me to teach lessons to brutes who were tormenting girls for the way they looked. Teenagers can be very cruel. I'd try to reason at first with these jackals. But invariably one of the bullies would come forward as if to start a pushing match. It never got to that. A challenger would have to penetrate my strike zone to shove me. Most of the altercations lasted only moments. The harassment always stopped.

I didn't always have to resort to the martial arts. Once I put a stop to a giant football player's habit of taking classmates' food in the cafeteria by bringing in some chocolate cupcakes I knew he'd demand. I laced them with Ex-Lax. It hit him later in math class. He ran out of the room in a panic. He never plundered another lunch box.

By the end of the ninth grade, I'd developed a reputation. Seniors quite a bit larger than me came gunning for action, but quickly learned the martial arts were more than just script material for movies and TV. My skills went with me on my visits to my cousins on Safie Drive. One night, my cousin, Stevie, and some other family members went to a go-cart track in the eastern suburbs. We were all wearing knee-length shorts. Soon some local teenagers were running their mouths, trying to instigate trouble.

"Hey, you camel jockeys," one taunted, slamming my heritage. "You need to change your clothes."

Stevie begged them to back off. "You need to drop this and go home," he said. "You really have no idea what you're dealing with here."

The local glared at me, walking forward. "You need to go home and get out of your pajamas," he said. "I don't like your shorts."

"If you don't like my shorts, you're really going to hate my shoes," I said.

"What is that supposed to mean?" he said as he crossed into my strike zone.

Stevie said later, "I'll never forget the look on that guy's face — that mixture of confusion, fear and the too-late realization that he'd tangled with the wrong guy as your foot came flying into his face."

Years later, I learned Stevie stopped telling me about any problems he was having with other students in his high school because he was afraid of what I'd do to them.

My role as an advocate for justice and self-defense wasn't always appreciated. In high school, another karate student and friend, James Croteau, and I were nearly expelled as the result of a martial arts rescue mission. School was letting out when we saw a student beating up a Spanish teacher just inside the school entrance. We pushed our way through a crowd of student onlookers. Soon the assailant was on the ground, writhing in pain.

That afternoon, we found ourselves sitting outside an administrator's office. I'd called our karate master to argue our case. We could hear Sam Santilli yelling behind the closed door.

"They told me that a teacher was being attacked, is that true?"

The administrator confirmed it.

"If you're expelling anyone, you're expelling the student who made the assault," he shouted. "And then you're going to go out there and thank my boys, and let the whole school know what they did was honorable."

And the administrator did.

Honor, however, was in short supply at home. My stepfather's drinking and tantrums only became worse, despite my mother's efforts to appease him. It was only a matter of time before my self-defense zone would expand in both physical and psychological proportions.

It happened not long after I started high school. Friends of my parents were in the house that night — a local minister, his wife and a couple of other dinner guests. My sister had just returned from a weekend ski trip. My stepfather had been drinking all night. I was lying on my bed, but I could hear the conversation at the table. My stepfather was picking on my sister. He wanted to know about a boy also on the trip.

"Did you play with his penis?" he asked her.

I couldn't believe my ears. I poked my head out of my bedroom door, yelling "What did you ask her?"

He repeated it.

"What are you saying?" I shouted.

"She's a little whore," he said. He stood up from the table.

I covered the distance down the hallway to the kitchen in hardly a second. When I arrived I was airborne, my foot extended. The flying side kick sent him crashing against the large kitchen table, flipping it over and sending food and dishes everywhere.

I stood over him. I was hardly five-and-a-half feet tall, but the giant had fallen.

"Apologize," I screamed, angry tears running down my cheeks. "Apologize to my sister, *now*."

He pulled himself to his feet and made the apology.

He never humiliated any of us again. For the next year he spent many of his evenings in his little basement prison with his vodka. My mother left him late in my senior year. We lived in a local motel for a month so I could finish the school year in Plymouth.

The doctor died years later, but his impact did not. If only I could have buried my anger with him. It would take many years to put that in its own unmarked grave.

CHAPTER 7

IMMATURE ENTREPRENEUR

I never had an aversion to work. I hungered for a future, perhaps because life with my stepfather was so unbearable. Work meant money, and money meant some independence. The idea of asking my stepfather for money appalled me.

In high school, I'd go to Safie Drive to visit with family on weekends. One of my older cousins, John Safie, had a small waterproofing business.

"C'mon out, Bernie, and we'll dig some basements," he liked to say. He taught me how to waterproof basement foundations and divert the sources of water coming from faulty roof designs and damaged downspouts.

My first job outside my family was that of a busboy at a Big Boy restaurant when I was in the ninth grade. Soon I became a cook, and finally head cook. I could flip two burgers at once, which didn't seem all that hard but appeared to impress a lot of my fellow employees. When I was 18, another restaurant hired me where I worked as a bartender for a short time.

My father, who remained totally involved in my life, wanted me to go to college right out of high school, but I was in too much of a hurry. Four years in classrooms seemed like a waste of time. But I also found that working for someone else was not completely satisfying. I didn't like the idea of my worth being limited to the figures on a paystub. I wanted to be in charge of my own destiny. I didn't like the idea of someone being able to fire me.

Indeed, I was fired from a job not a year out of high school, but not without learning a valuable truth. The greatest opportunity comes not necessarily when you're hired, but when you lose a job. When you're working for someone else, most of your time belongs to your employer. When you lose a job, you not only have the opportunity to find a better one, you free up time to pursue your own dreams. I define a job as "just over broke."

This lesson unfolded after my mother began dating a painting contractor named Gus, who hired me to work for him. I spent my mornings with paint, brushes and rollers. Then, at noon, he'd often take me to his business lunches where he'd negotiate painting deals. He was a major contractor, his accounts including some of the top corporations in Detroit. For example, I painted the office of former Chrysler Corporation Chairman Lee Iacocca.

Watching Gus negotiate multimillion-dollar contracts over lunch was fascinating. Dealmaking looked and sounded so easy. I'd always assumed big business negotiations were very formal, a secret art known only to a privileged few. No, they involved talking — friendly, casual talking. And listening. Gus listened to prospective customers. He first determined their needs, then displayed a confidence that he could meet them.

On the romance front with my mother, however, Gus turned out to be very possessive. He wanted her to fly to Greece with him and get married. When she declined the proposal, they broke up and Gus fired me immediately.

I decided I would keep painting. I'd negotiate my own deals, I told myself, finding jobs on a much smaller scale. But what the hell, I'd already seen how it was done.

Over the years, Stevie Safie and I had remained very close. We still had the dream of going into business together. I was always brimming with ideas, but I often got ahead of myself. Once, while I was working at Big Boy, we'd talked about opening a restaurant together.

"It started with one restaurant," Stevie later told a friend. "But by the end of the conversation Bernie had a national chain going, complete with a centrally located training center."

This time, my idea was painting. I also was thinking ahead toward general construction work as I designed my first business card. It showed a paintbrush swiping color across "Pavoné Construction, Inc." Commercial. Residential. Industrial. Bernie Pavoné, President. I was 18 years old.

Stevie had ideas of his own, too — good ones. We'd seen our uncles buy older, run-down properties, fix them up and either sell them or rent them for a respectable profit. Stevie and I wanted to buy real estate and put our little construction company to work on our own investments. He drove around Mt. Clemens, scouting potential buys. He found a duplex, its owner anxious to move to a new neighborhood. We met with the owner and offered him a land contract, no money down. He took it. How and why a property owner would trust two young men hardly out of high school to make good on their promises seemed almost unbelievable. But even then, we had the gift of gab. After the closing, we went to work on the property with paint, new fixtures and general repairs. Soon, we had two tenants and a cash flow.

Our second purchase was even more fortuitous. We were scouting a property in downtown Mt. Clemens when a group of young women, our age, waved to us from across the street.

"You guys moving into the neighborhood?" one inquired.

"We're looking for property to buy," I said.

"Why don't you buy mine?" one asked.

That night Stevie took her out. He called me the next day with the whole story. The woman had inherited the house, but couldn't keep up with the maintenance, mortgage payments and taxes. The bank was taking action to foreclose. The house was in need of repairs. She just wanted to stay in the home, but didn't want the hassle of owning it.

"You sign over the house to us, and we'll take care of everything," I told her. "In return, you will only have to pay rent, and you'll always have a place to live."

She sold the property to us for a dollar. We picked up $17,000 in equity when she transferred the title.

A few months later, we bought a building in New Baltimore, a three-unit commercial property with a trophy shop, a dry cleaner and a pizza shop as tenants. Like all the other properties, the building needed painting and repairs. Most of all of it needed waterproofing. The basement leaked like a sieve. Other buyers had passed on the property because of an expected $10,000 in foundation repairs. We rolled up our sleeves and accomplished the job for less than $500 — all for materials.

Leaky basements. They were everywhere in a state where low

pressure fronts glide across the Great Lakes and unleash torrential downpours three seasons out of the year. We had a track record waterproofing. So Stevie and I started a waterproofing business, too, using photos and examples of our work from our own properties for marketing.

Each job produced another job. If you do good work, if you keep your promises, word-of-mouth becomes a more powerful sales tool than Yellow Pages ads or freeway billboards. Soon, we were hiring crews. Stevie supervised the jobs while I made sales calls. As jobs came in, I would get calls asking if I did roofing.

"Certainly," I'd tell the customer.

I'd go to the Yellow Pages, find a roofing contractor and ask a representative to meet me at the house. I'd negotiate a good price subcontracting the job, mark up the roofing estimate to the customer, and make a small profit.

At first, I loved the business. It was a great way to make money, but I wanted to get bigger. Any time I touched anything, I wanted it to become bigger than life. I wanted to make sure we continued to grow and that we supported our employees.

Stevie wanted to move more slowly. He also resented being stuck on the jobs with the laborers, while I drove around all day negotiating deals. After a year, we parted but there were no hard feelings. We just had different visions. In 1986, he started SAS Basement and Waterproofing, which was very successful in southeast Michigan. I went to work starting a second company. (I never enjoyed the waterproofing part of the business.) I wanted a name that sounded high tech — a *system*. "The Hydroseal System," I called it. And I offered a lifetime guarantee.

The name clicked in the metropolitan Detroit market. I attracted substantial business from established contractors who had long-standing reputations in the community. My strategy: Advertise in their market and underbid their prices. Most were charging customers at an 80 percent profit margin. It was easy to undercut their prices.

Before my old high school classmates had even graduated from universities, I sometimes earned $30,000 a month. By some people's standards, I'd arrived. I was able to easily support my mother. We moved into a modest, three-bedroom ranch home in Plymouth. I drove a Mercedes and had plenty of cash for clothes and nightlife. I impressed a lot of people, but not necessarily my father.

"You need to get an education, Bernadino," he kept saying.

"College?" I said. "Dad, I'm making more money in a couple months than the teachers make in an entire year."

But finally, I enrolled at Schoolcraft College, which had a two-year program in business administration. I did it simply to please him.

That's not to say I did not want to broaden my horizons. Despite the money I was making, I found myself dissatisfied. I wanted to build a business that was unique, one that could expand across the country. I wanted to create an exciting enterprise that my entire extended family would find irresistible and want to join and share in the wealth.

In retrospect, I know I was trying to recreate the best memories of my boyhood. I'd never forgotten the joy of working and playing with my cousins during the summer on Safie Drive — those days that so rapidly fell away when my parents divorced and my cousin, Georgie Safie, died.

I wanted to recapture the innocence of my childhood. And I

decided that neither studying at a university nor waterproofing a thousand leaky basements would ever get that done.

CHAPTER 8

BRIGHT LIGHTS, BIG CITY

With a big, steady cash flow, I had the money to live a little. In fact, I lived a lot.

It was the eighties — the Decade of Greed as some called it. It was the end of junk bonds, insider trading and a steadily climbing Dow. The booming Reagan years were on, and with it the appropriate perks: Rolex watches, BMWs, GQ fashions, and slim women in tight, carefully pressed Calvin Klein jeans. Professional sports and nightlife became diversions. Developers built plush skyboxes in stadiums. Yuppies angled for courtside seats in the suddenly popular NBA. Jazz and blues clubs became hot. Dance clubs were packed. It was "Flashdance" and Michael Jackson and a new Saturday night fever, this one stoked by the young white collar crowd's discovery of cocaine. Las Vegas came roaring back from the doldrums of an aging Rat Pack and the misery index of the Carter years. New resort hotels sprang up. Sports betting boomed. The desert town had begun its transformation to the entertainment destination for many Americans. I loved Vegas. I loved to play at the tables. I loved to fly to Vegas for the big fights and hang out with the new money crowd. I've always had a talent for getting on the inside track. Maybe it's because I'm outgoing and care about people. But being too forward also can easily be perceived as being aggressive or manipulative. For me, the key has always been to be gracious and genuine. Put the other person first. Find out what the other person needs and find a way to fill that need. Some people will no doubt take advantage of your generosity. But many more will return the favor tenfold.

What I saw as my next big break happened in Las Vegas in 1988.

I flew to Las Vegas with a cousin, *Johnny Fredo.* One night at a craps table, I was up $10,000 when Johnny bet against me. Soon, I lost the ten grand and an additional $2,000.

Later, while we were waiting at the airport for the trip back to Detroit, I gave Johnny hell.

"Johnny, you're family. How could you do that?"

We were bantering back and forth when a man, who apparently had been listening to us, approached.

"I was at your table and I made a lot of money off your roll."

He gave me his business card. His name was Pasquale *"Pat" Caluzzi* and he owned a nightclub in Chicago.

I stared at his card cradled in my hand. Then, *the idea* hit me, an idea that would take hold of me for several years.

A nightclub. A kick-ass nightclub.

Of course, I thought. That's it. A national chain of nightclubs.

I did not know anything about nightclubs, their operation or design but I knew what I would want. I remembered evenings listening to the Beatles in Georgie Safie's room.

"Twist and Shout."

That would be the theme; an eclectic mix of music and cinema and pop culture from the early rock era.

I pictured a big record for a dance floor. I envisioned a huge DJ booth in the shape of a 1958 Corvette with the hood up and the DJ working out of it.

I thought about animated, life-size figures: Marilyn Monroe on a street vent, her dress being blown up like in the famous movie scene. Clark Kent standing in a phone booth. Every thirty seconds he'd open his shirt and expose the "S." I pictured Superman on a wire. The DJ could push a button and the Man of Steel would whoosh through the lasers and lights overhead. That could signal a "Super Shot Special," with waitresses on roller skates serving the crowd with one-dollar shots.

Fun, animated, high energy. That's the way it would be on the inside.

Outside, I could see King Kong hanging on the building and a revolving globe on the roof proclaiming:

"ROCK THE WORLD."

And I could rock it. I could take care of guests and network with patrons. I could make introductions and help facilitate business between young people with bright ideas. I could bring my cousins and friends aboard a business like that — a business dedicated to having a good time.

Little did I know that day in the Las Vegas airport I was about to begin a journey that would consume me for the next four years. It all began with a question. Great successes can begin with a question.

But so can great disasters.

I looked up from the business card and turned to the Chicago entertainment entrepreneur.

"So, Mr. Caluzzi, what can you tell me about the nightclub business?" I asked.

While strategizing on the nightclub project, I made another trip to Vegas the following year. I was sitting in a restaurant at the airport relaxing at a table near a big screen TV tuned into the NBA finals. Standing on the other side of the restaurant was a man with his date. His eyes were straining to see the game on TV.

I walked over, telling him: "You're really into the game. Why don't you and your guest take my table?"

"What about you?" he asked.

"I'll stand somewhere else."

"I can't do that," he said.

"Then please join me."

We introduced ourselves and exchanged business cards. He was Don Guiliano, the Vice President of Promotions for Caesar's Palace — a big title at a big casino. We talked for awhile and I mentioned that I wasn't very interested in basketball but I loved boxing.

When I got up to leave, he extended a surprising but very welcome offer.

"When you want to see a fight at the Palace, you just call me from now on, OK?"

I took him up on his offer, calling his office, a few months later. Detroit's Tommy "The Hit Man" Hearns was scheduled to fight Sugar Ray Leonard for the middleweight title at Caesar's Palace in June, 1989 and I wanted to see the fight.

"You come on out," Guiliano said. "Leave the rest to me."

When I arrived at my hotel in Las Vegas, media credentials were waiting. My press pass gave me access to the final workouts and a ringside seat with the press corps. During the training sessions, both fighters made eye contact with me. I don't know who they thought I was. I was wearing a nice suit and a tie. But I hardly looked old enough to be a promoter.

The fight itself was a classic. Both fighters pounded each other incessantly with huge blows. Leonard successfully defended his title. The contest lasted only three rounds, but is considered one of the greatest slugfests in boxing history.

Afterward, I went to a place called the Shark Club. Shortly after I arrived, Hearns, Ray "Boom Boom" Mancini, Marvin Hagler and several other fighters came in. A few minutes into the party, Hagler sent over one of his bodyguards, who took me to meet Hagler.

"You were at ringside while they were warming up," Hagler said. "Who are you?"

"Bernadino Pavoné," I said. "I'm from Detroit."

"Are you with Kronk?" he asked, referring to the Detroit gym where Hearns trained.

I shook my head. "I'm in martial arts. I trained under Master Willie Adams and Master Sam Santilli."

"Adams?" Hagler said, raising his eyebrows. "That man is a legend. That's great, man. That's really great."

Minutes later, Hearns approached me with similar questions. Hearns not only knew Adams, but Santilli, too.

"They both used to train me," Hearns explained. "I had bad hands. They helped me strengthen them."

I wanted Hagler to know how much I appreciated the conversation, so I sent him a bottle of Dom Perignon champagne. For the next hour or so we put quite a dent in the bottle and two or three others.

The Vegas trip, seeing one of the great fights in boxing history and meeting Hearns and Hagler, of course, were moments I have never forgotten.

But now it was time to pursue the *idea.* The pursuit would consume me and develop into a compulsion that almost ruined me forever.

CHAPTER 9

NIGHTCLUB TURNED NIGHTMARE

I was already thinking of the grand opening and working on a guest list in my mind. I called my father and said, "Dad, we're going to get you an Armani tux — an Armani and some beautiful dress shoes. That's the kind of grand opening it's going to be."

"Twist and Shout" was still only an idea, but I already had the spotlights in the sky. I asked myself: How hard could it be to locate property, formalize the design and put together a group of investors for the first club?

I formed the American Entertainment Management Group and went to work. I figured it would cost about $800,000 to open the first nightspot. I traveled regularly to Chicago on weekends to meet with potential investors arranged by Caluzzi and to inspect new clubs. I stayed in the presidential suite at the Marriott which was more spacious than my home in Plymouth.

Caluzzi introduced me to one particularly promising prospect. The potential investor wanted me to raise more capital, find a location, get permits, and handle all the other legwork. When the club was completed and operational, the investor would be entitled to 50 percent of the profits. That sounded fair to me. I could share the wealth, at least initially. But the investor wanted me to get the preliminary work done in Detroit before he'd make any funds available for construction.

In Chicago, I discovered a beautiful nightclub called Gatz 223. I fell in love with the fresh and innovative design. They gave me the designer's name, a company out of Dallas, Texas, and I called the firm immediately.

"We happen to be working in Livonia (Michigan) right now, designing a club," an executive told me. "It's in a Holiday Inn."

The hotel was only a few minutes from my Plymouth home and I met with the designers. The nightspot they were working on was called Tremors, which eventually opened as a world-class dance club. I told them about my plans and retained them. Their design, based on my "Twist and Shout" concept, eventually would cost $52,000.

I found property in Detroit's warehouse district, an area along the waterfront of the Detroit River just east of downtown. Several blues and jazz clubs were already established in the area. The warehouse I leased had all the right specifications for the design. It was a perfect building in a perfect location.

Surely, now, I thought, investors would come aboard. Instead, the people I'd been working with in Chicago dragged their feet. They wanted me to raise capital in Detroit before making a commitment.

I learned some hard lessons. All dealmaking wasn't as straightforward as the construction business. "Yes" didn't always mean *yes*. "Yes" could also mean: "I'm telling you yes so you'll be appeased and I won't have to put any strain on myself, but what I really mean is, no, I'm not doing it." Those kinds of mixed messages cost me months of pursuing meaningless leads. I learned to value someone capable of straight talk. I made myself a promise that I would never deal with people that way. It's a promise that helps form the backbone of ICR Services.

As the project moved along, my attention to the construction business faltered. Soon, waterproofing was generating little cash flow. There were more expensive trips to Chicago. I spent money lining up potential investors in Detroit as well. Interested affluent friends in Plymouth made promises and said they were ready to go. One put up $20,000, and another $17,000, and told me there was more to come. One may have been more interested in my mother than in the nightclub. His involvement never panned out, and I paid back the money I owed him.

My cash was dwindling. The lease on the building near downtown was $7,000 a month. But I continued spending on business entertainment, often using credit cards. I spent $30,000 alone at one nightclub where I liked to entertain prospects. I always picked up the tab; I thought that was the way business had to be done.

My sister, Theresa, wanted me to think smaller. "Bernie, you've got a building," she said. "Let's put $25,000 or $50,000 into it and just get in there. Let's make some money and then after a year, we'll renovate and reopen."

The club's debut had to be big — and perfect — I told her.

As the months passed, I incorporated other strategies. City officials indicated urban development funds were available to match me dollar for dollar on my first club. I hired a Detroit-area attorney named Wade McCree to secure a zoning variance allowing a nightclub on the site. I had my liquor license in place and parking to qualify for the zoning, which I had worked out with the adjacent building owner. I paid $1,600 for tickets to a mayoral fundraiser, hoping to facilitate city cooperation.

I also pursued other real estate deals. When I heard a $1.6 billion expansion was being considered for Detroit Metropolitan Airport, I purchased a five-acre parcel nearby and convinced my father to buy an adjacent parcel. I negotiated his purchase as well.

But my main priority was the nightclub. To stay in that game, I borrowed money from my father, my mother, and my sister. I sped from one business meeting to another in a leased Mercedes, the blueprints for "Twist and Shout" in my trunk.

I accumulated speeding tickets. Wade McCree represented me on the traffic violations, but I couldn't beat all of them. Moving violations earned "points" in Michigan — two points for five over the speed limit, for example. Reach 12 points and the state suspended your license. I was always just one violation from the 12-point threshold.

By the late 1980s, the fear of failure was driving me. I was mired in preserving my image and procrastinating on tough decisions. It's a memory that has never left me, and I see the same state of mind in people all the time. I try to coax people to step back to take a good rational look at what they're doing. Get your day planned. Get it organized, and then do the most important thing first. Get all the facts, make the hard decisions and act on them — and do it now!

But back then, that kind of practical approach was beyond me. Credit cards became my solution. They allowed me to purchase clothes, dinners and other amenities in a lifestyle fit for a successful nightclub owner. But I *was not* a successful nightclub owner. In fact, I was broke.

One day, when I was still pursuing the nightclub in the warehouse district, a homeless man asked me for money on the street.

"If I give it to you, what are you going to do with it?" I asked. "Are you going to buy something to eat or something to drink?"

He said he was hungry. I handed him a couple dollars, but told him to meet me the next day and I'd buy him lunch. He showed up the next day and we went to a local restaurant. We struck up a friendship and frequently I'd hand him a $20. I felt a haunting affinity to the man.

One evening, I saw him on the streets and took him to another restaurant a block from the warehouse. I was well known in the restaurant and knew the owner.

"They'll never let me in," the homeless man said.

I laughed. "They think you're a bum from the streets, but nobody knows my story. I'm losing my whole deal down here. I'm on my last legs. Soon we're going to be on the streets together. Besides, I know the owner."

We walked into the bar, but the bouncer stopped my raggedly dressed guest. I summoned the owner who let us in, but gave orders to the staff not to serve a drink to my friend. The owner disappeared into the kitchen. I decided we'd go elsewhere.

As we walked out, the bouncer glared at me and said, "Keep your nigger out of here from now on."

I stopped. "What did you say?"

He pulled his arm back to show the gun in his holster and repeated his earlier insult, adding, "or I'll blow your head off."

I was five feet away. My instinct was to throw the bottle I had in my hand as hard as I could. I did, hitting him in the forehead.

He crumbled to the floor, unconscious.

Two days later I was called down to police headquarters. The bouncer had pressed charges, claiming I'd assaulted him. I explained what happened to a black police sergeant.

"There's no case here," he said.

There may have been no case, but my attack on the bouncer was a telling sign of how stressed I'd become. I didn't like the consequences of my own decisions. For the first time in my life, my ideas seemed to be going nowhere. My solution of credit card spending also was turning into a problem. I'd always had impeccable credit. Now, I found myself making late payments on bills.

The impact didn't hit me until I went to lease a Lincoln at a Ford dealership. The salesman was a high school friend. As I sat at his desk, he looked over my credit report and laughed.

"Bernie, you couldn't qualify for a Pinto let alone a Lincoln," he said.

I asked to see the report. He said he couldn't show it to me under the rules. I made a big scene and finally the sales manager showed me the report. My credit was shot. My late payments were noted, but I also saw other information that was flat-out wrong. I contacted my attorney Wade McCree, who told me about a law called the Fair Credit Reporting Act. The law was designed to remedy what appeared to be a flawed reporting system, but it was complicated and time-consuming. Nevertheless, I obtained a copy of the statute and studied it.

By 1990, the Detroit nightclub plan collapsed in a tangle of city bureaucracy and empty promises. The financing the city had promised was instead given to another theme nightclub chain on the waterfront. I finally got out of the lease, but I still refused to give up on the plan for a nightclub. I decided I'd take the concept to Pontiac, a city 30 miles north of Detroit. The location would be easily accessible to potential clubgoers from Detroit's affluent suburbs. Surely, I could sell the concept in Pontiac.

I decided to go to a network marketing convention in Colorado, searching for new opportunities. In Colorado, I received two more speeding tickets and lost my license for two years. I hired a teenager who lived around the corner from my house to drive me to my meetings. I had a 1988 Mercedes and a driver — two luxuries I clearly couldn't afford.

Despite my troubles, my creative energies never stopped. My mind was always active.

For instance, I had trouble with my gums because, as a teenager with braces, I was taught to brush back and forth, causing my gums to recede.

As an adult, my gums would be sore after brushing and I asked my dentist for a special tooth brush which, he said, did not exist.

My mind went to work and over a six-year period I invented one.

I created the Orthodontic Toothbrush Company and during two years designed the kind of toothbrush I needed and received a patent for it.

Overall, the brush is designed to soften the stress on gums for people like me who have worn braces or who have very sensitive gums.

The toothbrush contains an elongated handle with a neck and head bristle design that promotes effective brushing while minimizing damage to gums. The outside rows are soft, long and angled at the ends, progressively shortening and stiffening as the move toward the center.

The key to my toothbrush is the center rows. They are positioned on a kind of shock absorber mechanism designed to reduce the pressure to the gums by deflecting bristles beneath the brace elements.

The toothbrush has not been manufactured nor was it marketed. But I have the patent and perhaps one day.

As to my immediate "business life," the airport property my father and I owned had great potential. But it would only gain value when the airport expanded years down the road. I'd borrowed $120,000 alone from my father and his wife, my stepmom. I signed over my airport property to him as collateral on my loan.

Also, after studying the credit law, I saw that consumers could challenge faulty information on their reports. Using the system, I was able to challenge and repair my own reports with the three leading reporting agencies. My mother became interested in the process. I corrected mistakes on her reports. Soon, relatives and friends were asking us to do theirs. But it never dawned on me that the service could become a major business.

By 1992, I had no cash flow and owed money to all my closest loved ones. I'd lost more than $400,000 pursuing the nightclub dream. It was no longer about the club. It was about me. All my self-worth was wrapped up into making it happen. I might have continued chasing the mirage, trying to make the possible out of the impossible, had it not been for a cop who helped me put on the brakes.

I was on my way to Pontiac for a big presentation, driving the Mercedes and carrying a driver's license I'd borrowed from a friend named Mario. I saw a Detroit police car parked on an expressway ramp when I passed it. In my mirror, I saw the car pull out to come after me.

I tried to lose the police cruiser. There were several exits and another freeway interchange nearby. I went up one ramp, turned on a surface street, and came down another. But the cop stuck with me. He pulled me over and approached the car, asking for my identification.

"Looks like you've lost a hundred pounds," he said, eying my friend Mario's license. Mario weighed 280 pounds.

He knew it wasn't me.

"Why are you in such a hurry, Mario?" he asked sarcastically.

I decided to come clean. "I'm in a hurry but, first of all, my name isn't Mario. It's Bernadino Pavoné and my license was suspended."

My moment of honesty didn't end with my speeding record. I found myself telling him how my plans for a nightclub in Detroit had failed.

"I'm broke," I said. "This car is going to be repossessed soon because I can't afford it. I just want you to know that I'm on my way to Pontiac for a meeting with some city officials."

"So, show me your plans," he said.

We went to my trunk. I pulled out a cylinder of blueprints, spreading the papers out on the hood. I pointed out the features of the club as hundreds of cars sped by not 20 feet away. I found myself detaching — looking at the scene of the two of us, me shouting my pitch over all that freeway noise.

This is insanity, I told myself.

When I was done talking, he looked me over. "Are you running late for your meeting?" he asked.

I nodded.

"So, tell me," he said. "How is driving 20 miles an hour over the limit going to get your club built any more quickly?"

I thought about it for a second, then looked him in the eyes. "Because I've been speeding for years," I said. "I lost my license chasing the deal. I've lost it all chasing the dream."

After a few seconds, he said "You know for some reason I believe you."

He directed me to drive to a nearby precinct. He followed me in his car. After we arrived, he asked me to wait in the lobby. He said he'd be off work in a few minutes and he had a solution for me. When he came out of his office, I thought he was going to arrest me. Instead, he asked for my keys and we walked to my car. He got behind the wheel and drove me to his house.

In the driveway he handed me my keys.

"I'm off duty now," he said. "It's no risk to me. You'll be the one taking the risk driving to Pontiac with no license. Does that sound fair?"

Tears started rolling down my cheeks.

"I wish you the best," he said. "And you know what, some day you're going to make it big."

I drove to the meeting in Pontiac. I was 45 minutes late, but still had time to make the presentation. Afterward, I felt different. For some reason that cop had given me a break. He could see something I could hardly see in myself anymore. I was physically and emotionally exhausted from running for four years on the wheel in a squirrel's cage. The only way to stop the wheel was to get off. If I did, I would have to face the question I'd been avoiding:

How in the world was I going to pay back all the money I owed to the people I loved the most?

CHAPTER 10

EMOTIONALLY BANKRUPT

I withdrew from everyone for a good six months. I stayed in my bedroom in the basement of the home my mother and I shared in Plymouth. I stopped shaving. I slept in late. I watched a lot of daytime TV.

My mother would roust me out of bed some mornings.

"Get up," she'd say. "Get your butt out of bed."

"Why?"

"Get a job. Do something."

"Do what?"

"Pump gas. Serve fast food. Anything. You need to get the hell out of this basement."

I'd roll over and adjust my pillow. She'd throw up her hands and storm back up the stairs.

She wasn't the only parent I believed I was letting down. I'd failed to get the college degree my father so highly valued. Over the years, I'd been haphazardly accumulating college credits for a business degree. I attended Schoolcraft College in the mid-eighties, then had enrolled at Eastern Michigan University to study marketing. But I took only one class in all of 1992 withdrawing from it early in the course. That year, my father was hospitalized for heart bypass surgery. I remember meeting my sister at the hospital after the procedure, telling her what the doctors had told me we could expect in the intensive care unit.

"He'll be hooked to all kinds of tubes, but he's doing much better than it looks, according to the doctors," I said. I wanted her to remain calm.

But when we walked into the unit I was the one who went into shock. He was unconscious, surrounded by monitors and life-support equipment. I fell to my knees and cried. I was convinced stress had damaged his heart. The money my father loaned me was part of his savings for retirement from Ford. My nightclub loan had prevented him from retiring when he planned.

His condition was my fault, I decided.

My mother, meanwhile, had taken a job as a district manager for a chain of upscale hair salons located in many metropolitan Detroit malls. She shouldn't have had to do that, I told myself. I'd spent all that money entertaining potential investors in Chicago and Detroit, and she was working in hair salons. My sister was helping support the household. The bank was threatening to foreclose on our house.

I felt responsible. I wanted to fix everything, but I didn't know how. Guilt finally dragged me out of bed and compelled me back into the basement waterproofing business, though not with the conviction and effort I'd demonstrated when I started the business. Soon, I had some jobs. This time I wasn't driving around town in a Mercedes chasing leads and developing new customers. This time I was on job sites up to my knees in the trenches.

I told myself, it would take years to pay back everyone at this rate. I couldn't seem to summon up that entrepreneurial spirit I had only a few years earlier — that belief that anything I did, I could do big.

One night, while sitting at home, the phone rang. It turned out to be a very important call. Picking it up would initiate a series of events that would forever change my life.

"Hey, Bernie, this is Mike," the voice said.

"Mike Kholer?" I asked.

When he said yes, I smiled. Mike Kholer was the younger brother of my best friend in middle school. He was the bright kid with the swimmer's physique and movie-star good looks. At one time he seemed to have everything going for him, but I hadn't heard from him in years.

"Where the hell you been?" I asked.

"I've been away," he said.

"Away where?"

The street definition of "away," he said. He'd been in prison for counterfeiting and armed robbery.

"What kind of counterfeiting?" I asked.

"You know, making American money, then you move it in Canada."

"No, I don't know, but that doesn't sound so good."

He also had been convicted of stealing $2,000 from a pizza franchise with a fake gun.

"Bernie, I just got out, and I'm on parole," he said. "Man, you know of any jobs? You got any work?"

I knew he would have a hard time finding a good job with a felony record. Yet, everybody deserved a second chance. I had always believed that and was willing to offer that, particularly to the brother of an old friend.

"Mike, you got it," I said.

"You sure?"

"We're doing construction and it's digging basements, you know, basement waterproofing, excavating. But if you can come by tomorrow, it's yours."

He showed up. We talked. I gave him the job.

Kholer turned out to be a productive addition to the waterproofing crew. He seemed eager to work and wanted to make money. He appeared motivated, so much so, that when he found out my mother worked for the chain of hair salons, he asked her if she had any moonlight work. She hired him to clean the salon after closing hours.

We hung out together as well as working side by side. I confided in Kholer the disastrous state of my personal finances. I worried out loud about owing my loved ones. We went out to nightclubs together and I introduced him to my friends.

A waterproofing job came up on a property in Dearborn, Michigan. The homeowner was a man in his 30s named *Hassan Batizi.* We chatted during breaks. He was friendly. We talked about my business and the need to keep jobs coming to pay my crew. I told him about the nightclub and how I'd spent my life looking for business opportunities. When we finished the waterproofing job, he was more than satisfied with our work.

A few nights later, Kholer and I went to the Baja Beach Club, a new upscale nightclub on the Detroit River waterfront, part of a national chain. I must have been a glutton for punishment. Baja Beach Club was a bitter reminder of my shattered dream. In fact, it was the very club that received the city financing I'd been unable to secure. Still, my own history aside, it was the happening nightspot on the riverfront at the time. I always wanted to be around people having fun.

I sat in my chair, talked with Mike and watched the crowd. The place was packed. I smiled and chatted with acquaintances but I could feel the grip of my lingering depression about my nightclub experience.

My eyes drifted toward the front door, and I recognized the man who'd just walked in. It was *Hassan Batizi*. He walked over to our table and sat down. We shook hands and made small talk. Then Batizi leaned back in his chair.

"Hey, Bernie," he said. "I got a job for you."

"Really," I said "Tell me about it." I figured he had a waterproofing lead.

Batizi looked around before asking me: "How would you like to make $100,000 overnight?"

I chuckled to myself. He must have had one hell of a big job and was looking for a finder's fee.

When I asked for details, he rose from his chair. He motioned me to follow him to a quiet corridor in the club. Looking back, I believe he was probably wearing a wiretap device.

"So, what's up?" I asked.

"You can make a hundred grand," he said quietly. "I mean, tonight — an hour's work."

I tilted my head, my eyes asking, doing what?

He continued, "It's a drug deal, man. All you got to do is deliver the shit, pick up the money and bring it to me. You're perfect for the job."

I was speechless.

"Look, it's a clean deal," he continued. "I know I can trust both ends. It's smooth. And something tells me I can trust you."

My mind flooded with questions. Trust me? Why? Because I was Italian? Because I was an Italian in the construction business?

I considered his offer an insult. I stepped closer, my nose only inches from his face. He wanted me to play the mobster role? I'd play it.

"Listen to me," I said. "Listen to me carefully because I'm not going to repeat it. You ever mention drugs to me again, I'll kill you? You got that?"

He looked shocked.

"I don't do dope," I continued. "I don't deal dope. And I don't like those who do."

He back peddled, holding up both hands. "No problem, man. Forget I ever said a word."

Seconds later, he disappeared into the crowd.

When I sat back down with Kholer, I was livid. "That guy is a pig," I said. "Where the hell does he get off thinking I'd go for something like that?"

"Easy, Bernie," Kholer said. "Relax."

But I fumed for a good five minutes. When I calmed down somewhat, I looked over at Kholer. He had a smirk on his face.

"What?" I asked.

Kholer smiled again, shaking his head. "You know, sometimes I'm so smart I scare myself."

"Smart?"

"Yeah, I got a great idea."

"Tell me," I said.

"How would you like to stick it to Hassan and make some serious money at the same time?"

"Talk to me," I said.

"Money," Kholer said. "Bogus money. And you know I know how to do it."

I should have given him the same treatment I gave Hassan Batizi minutes earlier. In retrospect, any interest I was about to express didn't make sense — logically or morally. I'd just been insulted by someone asking me to do something illegal. So the solution was to consider doing something illegal back?

But I was angry. And anger was doing my thinking now.

"You see, you print the money," Kholer continued. "And then you sell it to him for 30 cents on the dollar. He has all the risk. He has to unload it. And here's the best part. It will take Hassan down."

"I'm listening," I said.

"You can make the money for next to nothing."

He went into the details.

When he finished, I looked at the crowd in the club. People were dancing and laughing and having a good time. At that moment, I felt isolated, even with that large crowd around me. I needed money — a lot of money. That was my problem. Why was I even spending money with that massive family debt on my back?

I saw Batizi hunched over at a distant table, talking on his cellphone.

I stood up. "Stay here," I told Kholer.

I walked over and when Batizi saw me, his eyes lit up. He hung up his cell.

"Thought it over?" he asked, grinning.

"I've got something better," I said. "You interested in some counterfeit currency — 30 cents on the dollar?"

"You know what I'd use them for," he said.

"I'm not talking about your deal tonight," I said. "I'm talking later."

He grinned again. I thought he was simply greedy. Only many months later would I discover the great break I was giving him had nothing to do with the discount. Hassan Batizi had a criminal record and was working as a police drug informant. I was about to hand him some major leverage to solve his own legal problems with authorities.

"Yeah, I'm interested but, like I said, you know how I'd spend them. I thought you had a problem with that."

"No," I said. "That's *your* problem."

It was a good comeback on my part, but I couldn't have been more wrong.

CHAPTER 11

WRONG IS WRONG; RIGHT IS RIGHT

There's a line. Often, it's defined by our laws, the moral instruments which help us maintain a civilized society. Other times, the line between right and wrong is not so easily perceived. We must look inside and to God for guidance, deciding what action is the right thing to do.

In 1992, I also learned something else about the line between right and wrong: Once you cross it, it becomes increasingly easier to ignore it — that is, until all the consequences catch up to you. Then, if you're lucky, the resulting pain compels you to change, presuming you haven't already completely destroyed your life.

Mike Kholer and I pursued our plan to — quite literally — make money. That was another great piece of logical thinking on my part. Who in their right mind would trust a self-proclaimed counterfeiting expert whose previous work landed him in prison? I did, and in short, I was a fool.

Kholer said the bills could be made by scanning them with a computer and printing them with a quality color printer on "cotton bond paper." The Treasury Department has since made the method of counterfeiting more difficult by changing bill designs and implanting materials that are almost impossible to reproduce. At the time, Kholer said the method was virtually undetectable.

Hassan Batizi, meanwhile, called me regularly. He wanted to see samples of bills before he committed to any kind of deal. Soon, I had in my possession color copies of two $20 bills.

It was late winter when I met with Batizi at a restaurant in Dearborn, one of Detroit's western suburbs, to talk over our arrangement. He didn't show up alone. He had a friend, named "Ronnie," with him. I was angry he'd brought a third party without telling me and I should have left, but I didn't.

Ronnie wanted to buy money and he had a story.

"Here's what I'm looking to do," Ronnie said. "I have a deal going to float tons of bogus bills in Germany. When the Berlin Wall came down and Germany reunified, it got their currency so messed up, they don't know which end is up. So it's the perfect time. What I'm saying is, we need to move fast. How much money can you actually bring us in the next few days?"

"I guess I could deliver as much as you need," I said.

He wanted to see a sample.

I handed over my two counterfeit $20 bills.

Later, I learned it was all being recorded on hidden video. Ronnie was a Secret Service agent. Court records later showed that the federal agency had been tipped off by local police who were tipped off by none other than Hassan Batizi. In Batizi's world of deal and tell, I was a big prize. That's why he was smiling that night at the Baja Beach Club. With my offer, I'd given him a lead to land a federal case.

Negotiations ensued. Promises were made. I would get a $10,000 deposit on a package of $50,000 in counterfeit bills. I told Ronnie I needed more time.

After my meeting with Ronnie, I remember lying in my bed that night at home, thinking how crazy it all was, how wrong it all was. But the next morning I got up and looked for a color laser printer that could print top quality images at a productive speed.

I'd promised to deliver more samples of the money six days after my first meeting with Ronnie. But a week later, I was still looking for a good printer. One day, as Mike Kholer and I drove around looking for the equipment, I sensed we weren't alone.

"Mike, I have this feeling we're being followed," I said.

He appeared unconcerned. "Man, you're paranoid," he said.

I switched lanes on the freeway. The car behind us switched lanes.

I got off the next exit and pulled into a Taco Bell. I walked over to a phone booth pretending to make a call. The car following us pulled in. I walked over.

"You're following me," I said.

"I'm just getting tacos," the man responded.

He faked an Arab accent. Given my family's Syrian heritage, I could easily recognize a fake Arab accent.

"I'm going to write down your plate and find out who you are," I said boldly.

As I reached into my pocket for a pen, I spotted a small, blue bubble light dangling on a cord below his dash.

Other police surveillance crews that were watching me must have thought I was going for a gun. A half dozen cars sped into the lot and several agents surrounded me, their handguns drawn. They threw me down on the pavement.

"Don't shoot," I pleaded. "I'm unarmed."

They handcuffed me and Kholer and put us in police cars.

A half-hour later, I was sitting at a table in a small room at a local police department. Two Secret Service agents were shooting questions at me.

"We have you cold on these bills," one said. "But you might be able to make it easy on yourself."

Apparently, I'd been under surveillance for some time. The agents wanted to know about a friend of mine from an Italian family on the east side. They thought I was somehow involved with him. My friend had visited my house with his father's car.

"How do you know them?" one asked.

"I used to live on that side of town," I said. "I grew up with the guy."

The agents made me an offer. Apparently they thought the Italian family was part of organized crime network. With my Italian heritage, they probably figured I was in the Mafia, too.

"If you tell us everything you know about this family," one said, "you won't have to do any time. You'll be our witness."

I told them I wanted to call my attorney.

One of the agents cracked me on the side of the head with a phone book.

"Okay, tough guy, call your lawyer," he said.

After the call, I told them I was ready to tell them everything I knew about the family. They brought in a video camera to record my statement.

When it started rolling, I said, "All I really know is they're some of the nicest people I've ever met. What I like most about this family is that they do so much for charity."

And that really was all I knew. The agents were not happy.

"You're all done," one agent said. "You're doing time — lots of time."

Surprisingly, however, they let me go, as well as Kholer. Apparently they weren't done with their investigation. I'd forced them into acting before they wanted to by confronting the agent at the Taco Bell.

While I was being interrogated, I presumed Kholer was getting the same treatment in another room. He wasn't. Later, I found he'd chatted with agents, sipping a Coke. He was also working with the police in an effort to get his parole shortened.

Kholer had other secrets, it turned out. He was doing a little criminal moonlighting. There was a reason he liked working after hours cleaning up the hair salons my mother managed. He was stealing carbons of credit card slips from the shops. He used the numbers to buy clothes and gifts for his girlfriend, and then expanded his purchasing to auto parts, which he turned around and sold. He was having the goods shipped to a rental property I owned.

Neither my mother nor I knew about Kholer's fraud. But my mother knew something was wrong at the beauty salons. A woman called and said she had been charged for something she would never buy — a gross of spark plugs. She knew the problem originated in the hair salon because it was the only place she ever used that particular card. My mother called the police.

A local fraud squad was already working on the case because other women had complained to police about charges for auto parts on their bills. My mother's call expedited the investigation because the detectives could link all the cards to the salons.

Following my detainment and release, I met with an attorney about the counterfeiting investigation. He wasn't very hopeful.

"You've got a serious problem, Bernie," he said.

You'd think that would have slowed me down. Instead, I became more desperate and bold. In retrospect, I think I was like an alcoholic trying to drink his way to his bottom. I couldn't stop. Maybe if the consequences got bad enough, maybe somebody else would stop me. I'd crossed that line, and I couldn't get back all by myself.

Apparently I was sending out signals.

A few weeks after the Secret Service interrogation, an acquaintance who worked as a teller at a Detroit bank approached Kholer and me. One subject led to another during the conversation. He told us that he had access to the cards containing customers' signatures for their accounts. Using the cards, we could forge withdrawal slips for long inactive accounts. Federal insurance would cover the losses, he told us. No one would lose money.

Of course I knew that insurance money comes from somewhere. The public pays for everything. But raising money to erase my debts was the only thing important to me.

Kholer, my acquaintance and I went to my basement bedroom to trace the signatures. Kholer would go into the bank in various disguises. More than $16,000 was withdrawn and we split the money three ways.

I made a lot of bad decisions. I took cash advances at nightclubs where I was well known, using fraudulent credit card numbers supplied by Kholer.

Halloween night of 1992 I dropped by a club in a Detroit suburb. Many of the people were wearing costumes out but I was wearing a suit.

I was sipping a drink when another patron, who I later found out was an attorney, approached me.

"What are you supposed to be, a businessman?" he asked, laughing.

I didn't think it was funny. We exchanged a few more words. He reached out and put his hand on my jaw. I locked his arm with one hand and struck him with my other, snapping one of his teeth in half. Two months later, I would be posting bond in a suburban Detroit court because the attorney had pressed charges for aggravated assault.

Why had a I lost my temper again? Maybe his joke about the suit was all too telling. Yes, I was pretending to be a businessman. I was a failure. I'd become a criminal.

I was at war with the world again — not unlike those days in my stepfather's home years earlier. I later realized I'd never really dealt with that cauldron of anger still simmering from those teenage years. I should have had counseling, or found a support group.

Instead, I found trouble, or trouble found me.

Not four months after the Halloween incident, I took a girl I'd been dating for several months for a weekend in Traverse City, one of Michigan's finest resort cities. She was very insecure, often worrying other women would steal me from her. Imagined threats to our relationship would throw her into fits of jealousy. I figured a weekend away together would calm her unfounded fears.

We spent an evening drinking wine in a condo I'd rented for the weekend at a premier resort. We had plans to go out to a small club in the city. The night ended with her screaming and throwing things at me in our room, convinced I was looking for other women. The argument spilled outside, where three guys who were passing by assumed I was trying to hurt her. They tried to jump me, and I defended myself.

The police came and I was charged with assault and malicious destruction of property. On the advice of a Traverse City attorney, I pled guilty to the property charges, but the assault charges were dismissed. I spent 15 days in jail and paid for the damages my girlfriend had caused in the room.

My dive to the bottom only continued.

Later, that year, I met a woman named *Tina Jennings.* I fell in love with her, and would eventually ask her to marry me. But even a committed relationship couldn't calm me, let alone pull me from the maelstrom of my own making.

One January night, three friends and I went out drinking in a rock club in Farmington Hills, one of Detroit's northwest suburbs. I was very drunk. We left just before closing. But in the parking lot, one of my friends got into an altercation with several other club customers. I went to his aid when somebody pushed a bystander into me.

Drunk, I thought I was being assaulted. I struck him, sending him to a local hospital emergency room with his injuries.

Assault charges were filed.

Two months later, I visited a dance club I knew well in a northwest suburb. Once inside, I saw an old female friend whose sister I had dated. I kissed her on the cheek.

"How's your sister?" I asked.

"Doing good," she said.

Moments later, her boyfriend came over and I introduced myself.

"What were you doing kissing her?" he asked.

"I always kiss her when I see her; we're old friends." I answered. "Let me buy you two a drink."

The boyfriend stiffened his back. "She doesn't want a drink," he said.

I laughed. "How did you do that?" I asked. "You must be a ventriloquist. Relax."

He snapped, "I told you she doesn't want a drink."

"Look, I know she can speak for herself," I said. "I've probably known her for a lot longer than you."

"He gets a little bit jealous," my friend said smiling nervously.

I could feel the anger building inside me. Another control freak, I thought, another bully who has to push his woman around.

He made a couple insults and stepped forward.

"You're crossing a line you don't want to cross," I said. "You really need to relax."

"No, I'm going to kick your ass."

"Believe me, this is a bad time for you to be making those kinds of comments," I said.

"Bernie, please don't hit him," my friend said.

The boyfriend snarled at her, "You're worried about what he'll do to me? You better worry about what I'm going to do to him."

"You don't know Bernie," she pleaded. "He's a karate champion."

I shrugged. "That was a long time ago. Just let me get you a drink."

He swung at me, but he was slow. I hit him once, leaving him with his front teeth protruding through his upper lip. I looked down at my hand, then his face.

"Is that weird, or what? I never saw that happen before," I said. "Does it hurt?"

He was stunned.

I walked over to the bar, got him a shot and handed it to him."Now, how about that drink," I said. "You look like you need it. I insist."

He drank it a bit sloppily, but he managed. He left for a hospital emergency room where I later learned he received eight stitches. He filed assault charges with the local police department.

In the span of six months, I'd been jailed once in northern Michigan and now faced three assault charges in various Detroit suburbs.

But they were minor cases compared to what was coming.

It was a balmy morning in August when a squad of Secret Service agents and local police broke down the door to our Plymouth home. They charged in at dawn wearing masks and waving assault rifles and handguns.

My mother watched in shock.

I was sleeping in my basement bedroom. I woke up fighting back, thinking they were intruders. In seconds, I was in handcuffs when an agent read me my rights.

I was 28 years old. Finally, somebody had stopped me.

It was the best thing that could have ever happened to me at that point in my life.

CHAPTER 12

BITTERSWEET COMMENCEMENT

Seven months after my arrest, I pled guilty to counterfeiting, bank fraud and credit card fraud. I didn't put up a fight. I didn't go to trial. The fight was over, not only with the law, but the fight with myself that had been raging for many years.

The pending assault charges in local courts prompted a suggestion from my attorney, Christopher Andreoff, who had become a trusted friend as well as my legal counselor. He suggested that I attend anger management classes. In counseling, I discovered patterns in my thinking and behavior.

I learned anger was a natural reaction when someone felt threatened. My stepfather had been a major threat as I developed into a young adult. I'd responded first with anger and finally with physical blows. My martial arts skills had stopped his abuse. But that didn't mean physical force was always the appropriate solution to my anger. As a teenager, I'd been trapped in that household and had limited options. But as an adult, I had many choices. As an adult, I didn't have to put myself in those situations. And if a situation showed up, I had the choice to walk away.

I decided to plead nolo contendere — no contest — to all the assault charges, though I could have argued self-defense. I received probation. I wanted to be done with that part of my life.

I knew I had many amends to make, particularly to my loved ones. As I waited for my sentencing on the federal charges, I took a full load of classes at Eastern Michigan University, working toward that degree my father so cherished. It was the least I could do for him. I'd let him down horribly in every aspect of my life in the past two years.

On a chilly day in early March of 1994, I arrived for sentencing in the courtroom of U.S. District Judge Nancy Edmunds. Among those accompanying me were my mother, my sister, my fiancée, *Tina Jennings*, (to whom I was engaged a few months earlier) my friend James Croteau, and our longtime family confidant, Jerry O'Connor. The day before, Jerry had taken me to his church and we'd prayed together, asking God for mercy.

Though I could barely pay for his legal services, Andreoff had worked hard to convince the court I could turn my life around. A half-dozen people also wrote letters to the court supporting me as well, including Wade McCree, my attorney during the nightclub years, and an old family friend, Jerry Benefield, then president and CEO of Nissan Motors in North America.

My case was called. I walked forward and stood in front of the large bench.

Judge Edmunds asked if I wanted to say anything.

I apologized for hurting everyone. I told her I felt terrible remorse for what I had put my family through.

"My mother and father are honest people," I said. "They don't deserve the pain I've caused them."

Judge Edmunds announced my sentence: I would have to pay nearly $93,000 in restitution and I would spend two years in a federal prison.

I almost collapsed.

"I understand you're a student at Eastern Michigan," Judge Edmunds continued. "We're going to let you finish your studies so you can graduate, then you can surrender to the prison facility."

Still in shock, I thanked the judge.

A few minutes later, I splashed water on my face in the restroom and tried to clear my head. *Two years!* I couldn't imagine being locked up for that long. I dried my face. I looked at myself in the mirror. No, I had put myself in this situation.

I had no one to blame but myself.

When I left the bathroom, I saw the door to the judge's chambers. I buzzed the lock, it opened, and I slowly approached the clerk's desk inside. I want to get a message to Judge Edmunds, I told the clerk.

"Tell her thanks, that she has just saved my life," I said. "And tell her I'm going to show her that the system can work and I plan to return here one day to thank her again."

As I left the courthouse, I knew there was an important visit I had to make. My father did not know all the details of my case. Considering his bypass surgery, I tried to spare him the strain. But now, with two years of incarceration pending, I would have to tell him.

I drove to my dad's house with my fiancée. We sat and talked at the dinner table for a while. I told him some of the details.

"I'm so sorry about ruining our name and I'll work very hard to build that back," I said. "But, Papa, I have to go away for awhile."

"That's good, son, you need to get away from all this," he said.

He hugged me. "I'm here for you and I love you."

He walked to the kitchen sink and turned on the water. He began washing dishes. I followed him, realizing he really didn't comprehend what I was telling him. I couldn't seem to get the word "prison" out of my mouth.

"Papa, I need to tell you something," I said. "I'm really going away."

He shrugged his shoulders. "I did it when I was young. I moved away from my family. It will be good for you."

He turned off the water and wiped his hands with a dish towel. Our eyes met again.

"Listen to me, Papa," I said. "What I mean is I'm going to prison for two years."

He fainted. I caught him with my arms as he fell.

For a few moments, I thought I'd killed him, that he'd had a heart attack. But several seconds later, he came around. When he stabilized, he cried. I cried, too. It was the single most painful moment of the entire ordeal.

In many ways it was the most painful moment of my life.

The German philosopher, Friedrich Nietzsche, is often quoted as saying: "When you look into the abyss, the abyss also looks into you."

I've taken that to mean that the worst moments of our lives are the very times when we establish our character. It is during those moments that we make our choices. We can continue to do things in the same destructive ways that got us there — and get the same results. Or, we can try new ways, or reaffirm the core values that we abandoned somewhere along the way.

If there were any doubts about what I had to do to atone for what I had done with my life, they were washed away that day with my father at the kitchen sink.

Over the next few months, there were no more days and nights of isolation in my basement bedroom. I not only pursued my studies at Eastern Michigan with new vigor, I put the waterproofing business into high gear. I worked night and day. I solicited jobs. I worked with the labor crews. I generated nearly $60,000 in two months and I paid back the money I owed my mother and sister, and I paid off some of my debt to my father and step-mother.

In June, the day of the university commencement ceremony arrived and I received my diploma, a bachelor's degree in business, with a major in marketing.

It was an occasion most families would find joyous. Many students had sent out announcements. There would be parties and dinners where new graduates would discuss career plans with proud relatives. An atmosphere of celebration reigned as everyone filed into the large auditorium for the commencement.

I'd prepared for the graduation in other ways. Celebration wasn't in my plans. Besides waterproofing my mother's house in Plymouth, I put on a new roof, repaired cement, and finished the basement. I didn't want her to worry about those things.

I also bought a cap and gown for my cousin, Stevie Safie, my first business partner. I wanted him to sit with me during the ceremony. He wasn't a student at Eastern, but I didn't want to be alone with the hundreds of other graduates. I managed to sneak him in and slip his name into the roster listing graduates. He even walked across the stage and received a "diploma" when his name was called. At that point I wanted to be close to family. I needed family more than ever.

It was a bittersweet moment when the president of the university called my name and I walked up to accept my diploma from his hand. As I walked from the podium, I looked out to the section where my family was sitting. I could see my dad. He had a broad smile and his eyes were glistening.

I could see the ceremony had made my father very happy, but I'm sure he would have liked to see me finish college under different circumstances than the ones I faced that day. In a few days, he and everyone else in the family knew we'd be driving to Manchester, Kentucky to surrender to authorities.

Graduation meant I was going away.

Bernie Pavoné was born May 11, 1965 in Detroit, Michigan.

Bernie's mom and dad with friends and family at a party in a night club in Windsor, Canada.

At the time of Bernie's birth, the Pavonés lived in this house in Harper Woods, Michigan.

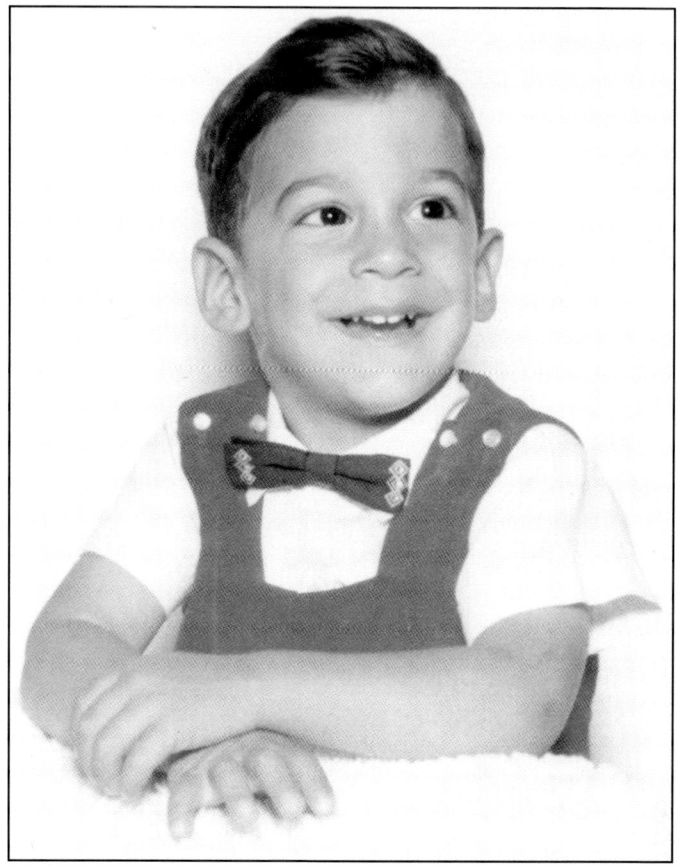

Bernie Pavoné at two years old.

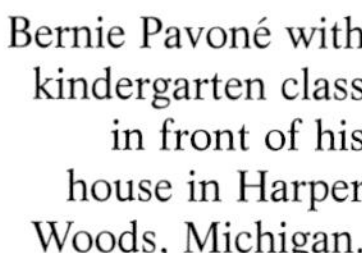

Bernie Pavoné with kindergarten class in front of his house in Harper Woods, Michigan.

"The Big House", where Bernie Pavoné spent much of his youth with relatives.

The Safie Pickle Factory where Bernie Pavoné learned important lessons about business.

The Beacon School where Bernie Pavoné attended the first and second grade.

Bernie Pavoné with his sister, Theresa, at a pool in Mt. Clemens, Michigan in 1973.

The Neil E. Reid Elementary School in Mt. Clemens which Bernie Pavoné attended for grades 1-5.

Relatives in the backyard of the "Big House," where they met to help Uncle George Safie in his campaign for state representative.

George Safie, who died in a tragic accident, pictured here with Bernie Pavoné's grandmother, Zbada Safie.

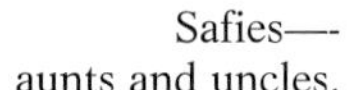

Safies—- aunts and uncles.

Home for Bernie Pavoné in Mt. Clemens at 23817 Fenton from 1973-77.

Nursing home which Bernie Pavoné and his sister, Theresa, along with their father, visited frequently to entertain patients with songs.

Given the dominance of the Safie family in a section of Mt. Clemens, George Safie won approval to name a street after the family.

Bernie Pavoné's middle school, L'anse Creuse South in Mt. Clemens, Michigan.

Bernie Pavoné shown here in the sixth grade in middle school, a picture he gave his mother with the accompanying note.

Home in Plymouth, Michigan during the difficult days with *Dr. Renee* from 1977-83.

West Middle School which Bernie Pavoné attended in Plymouth, Michigan from 1977-78.

Plymouth Canton High School attended from 9th-12th grades.

Bernie Pavoné in cap and gown at his high school graduation in 1983.

Home in Plymouth, Michigan where Bernie Pavoné lived at the time of this book's publication.

Bernie Pavoné takes his black belt karate test in Detroit, 1984.

Sparring with karate colleagues in gym.

Bernie Pavoné at graduation from Eastern Michigan University with his mother, Mrs. Gloria Tactac.

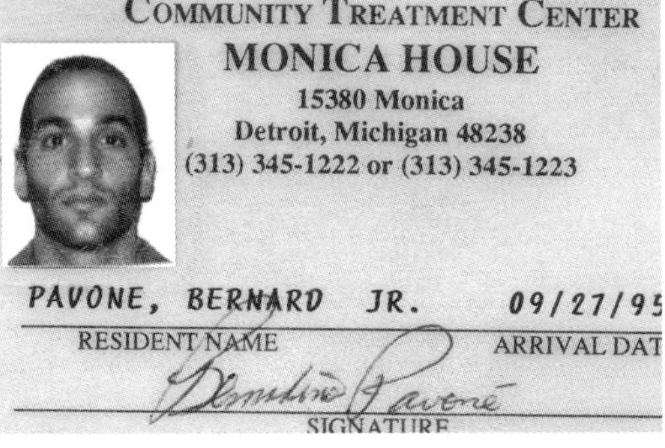

Three inmate cards (from top):

- Photo ID upon arrival at federal prison
- Photo ID just prior to release
- Photo ID while at half-way house

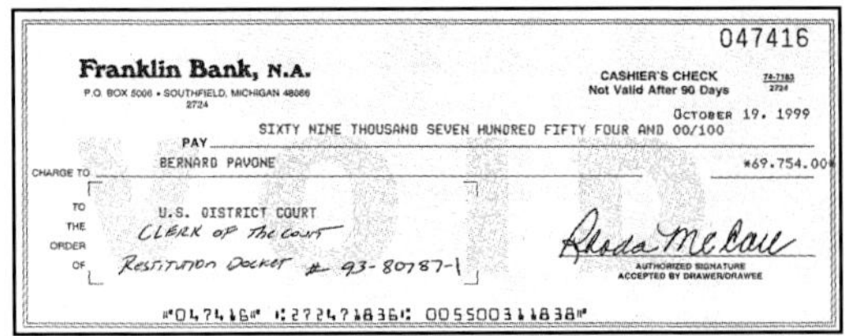

047416

Franklin Bank, N.A.

CASHIER'S CHECK
Not Valid After 90 Days

OCTOBER 19, 1999

PAY SIXTY NINE THOUSAND SEVEN HUNDRED FIFTY FOUR AND 00/100

CHARGE TO BERNARD PAVONE *69.754.00

TO THE ORDER OF U.S. DISTRICT COURT
CLERK OF THE COURT
Restitution Docket # 93-80787-1

AUTHORIZED SIGNATURE

A copy of the cashier's check covering the last payment of restitution the U.S. District Court ordered Bernie Pavoné to pay as part of his sentence.

Mrs. Gloria Tactac, Bernie Pavoné's mother, visits her son in prison.

Working with a front end loader on a prison detail in a state park.

Theresa with her brother in 1996.

The office building which houses ICR Services headquarters in Livonia, Michigan.

ICR Services' International Processing Center in Canton, Michigan.

ICR Services' Distribution Center in Los Angeles, California.

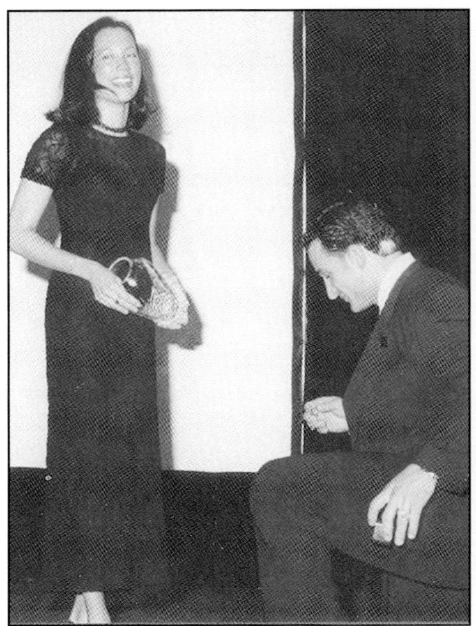

Marriage proposal to fiancée, Lisa, on stage in front of hundreds of ICR representatives at national convention in July, 1999.

Engaged couple celebrate the moment at national convention.

Friend and former legal advisor, Judge Wade McCree with Lisa and Bernie Pavoné.

Some of Bernie Pavoné's karate family at the 1999 grand national championships in Philadelphia. (Bernie Pavoné third from left)

On vacation in Monaco, 2000, with Lisa.

On vacation at the Coliseum in Rome.

Mrs. Gloria Tactac, ICR Services Chairman, Bernie Pavoné, Harmik Poghossian, ICR Services *Corporate Executive*, and Abood Samaan, ICR Services Co-Founder.

Bernie Pavoné Sr. with his second wife, Helen.

Mrs. Gloria Tactac's home in Bloomfield Hills, Michigan, which her son bought for her — as promised.

Mrs. Gloria Tactac with long-time family friend and confidant, Jerry O'Connor.

Mary Safie (center) in the pickle business which was restarted in 1994.

Night before Theresa's wedding in Rome, Italy. (Left to right): Steve Safie, waiter, Bernie Pavoné, Enzo Pavoné, Theresa's husband-to-be Tony Borello, and Sergio Aguero.

Theresa, who was married in the Vatican, shown here in front of a fountain in Rome, Italy. With her are (left to right): Sergio Aguero, Enzo Pavoné, husband Tony Borello, Bernie Pavoné and Steve Safie.

Celebrating Theresa's wedding in Rome, Italy.

Bernie Pavoné addressing representatives in Los Angeles at national convention in June, 2000.

The Villa Flore Estate in Sacramento, California, which is used for executive conferences.

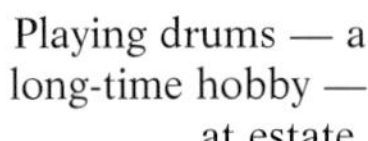

Playing drums — a long-time hobby — at estate.

Bernie Pavoné "jamming" at estate with Charlie Rashid and Abood Samaan.

ICR Services, Inc. Co-Founders:
Bernadino Pavoné, President and CEO
Mrs. Gloria Tactac, Chairman
Abood Samaan, Chief Strategy Officer

CHAPTER 13

SURVIVING FCI

I hadn't been in FCI Manchester two hours when a man, about 30, walked up to me while I was waiting in a corridor to be assigned to my first holding cell.

"You look Italian," he said.

I nodded. "Half Italian, really. Syrian, too."

"Hey, I'm half Italian, too. I'm from Venezuela."

I introduced myself.

"My name is Sergio," he said. "Sergio Aguero."

He looked at me for a few moments, then added, "Someone wants to meet you."

"Me?"

"His name is Ciccio. He's my friend. I will introduce you."

I was curious about the interest in me, but apparently Sergio's friend had seen me arrive, and for some reason, wanted to meet me.

Sergio walked away. Moments later, the guards directed me to the mess hall, a room divided between blacks and whites. I had no clue as to the lay of the land in this prison environment. But when in doubt, I always tend to go against the grain. I sat with the blacks and made small talk. No one insulted me; in fact, some were friendly.

As I ate, I noticed a distinguished-looking white man in his fifties sitting at one of the tables on the other side of the room. Several inmates seemed to go out of their way to greet him. Others were giving him some of their food.

I was walking away from my table when Sergio came up to me and said, "I'll come down and get you tonight. You'll meet my friend."

That night, as I lay on my bunk, the reality of where I was began to sink into my consciousness. Other new inmates in my holding cell bickered over bunks and housekeeping. There was a lot of posturing going on. It all seemed so trivial. Then Sergio showed up at the open cell door.

We walked down the corridor and entered an open cell.

"This is Ciccio," Sergio told me as he introduced me.

My eyes fell on the face of the man who I'd seen receiving all the deference earlier in the mess hall.

"Sit down," Ciccio said. His Italian accent was very thick.

I hesitated.

He motioned with both his hands. "Please, I want you to sit down."

As we talked, he said he was from Sicily.

"I'm in here for 35 years," Ciccio said, who was 53.

He didn't say why and I didn't ask.

I was so emotional from my first hours in prison I just opened up, telling him about my family, and how I'd let them all down.

He listened quietly. When I finished, he said in his thick accent, "People in here can be vultures. I'm gonna look after you to make sure you're all right."

That apparently included telling Sergio to educate me. Sergio spent a lot of time at my side in the days ahead. Sergio said because I was doing far less time than most other inmates, that would make me an object of envy. He told me people and places I should avoid, suggested where I might want to work, and even told me the questions my counselor would ask.

The first concept I had to grasp was that prison was a very petty place. Pettiness often could be carried to dangerous extremes. A disrespectful look, a rumor — these and many other minor impressions, real or imagined, could add up to big trouble very quickly.

In some ways, navigating the poisonous attitudes of fellow inmates could be even more difficult in a medium-high security facility like FCI Manchester. High security prisons have more rigid rules and highly regulated lock-downs. But in Manchester, inmates worked and socialized with each other during the day. In the evenings, individual cells remained open.

"If someone wants you, they can find you," Sergio said.

The only real protection was the solitary confinement section known as "the hole," but that was no easy place to do time.

The so-called "country-club" federal facilities may be reasonably safe. But the two facilities where I would be housed over the next 18 months had plenty of career criminals who would make it difficult for me to do my time.

I told Sergio I wanted to stay out of trouble, get released and go on to live a normal, law-abiding life. But some career criminals would resent that because they wouldn't be getting out any time soon, he said. Some would try to instigate conflicts with insults or petty issues. If I fought and was caught, I would lose my "good time" and a chance at early release. It was a no-win situation, Sergio said, and the troublemakers tried to play that to their advantage.

For those who really got caught up in the mind games, I learned the results could be deadly. In a state without the death penalty, no additional punishment could be given to a lifer. Even if one was caught committing a murder, he'd still get lunch that day.

It was the reality behind bars, Sergio explained.

The weapon of choice was the "shank." Men with hate in their hearts and time on their hands could make a shank from almost any metal object. They fashioned them in the metal shop from stolen scrap metal. Those with no shop access would spend countless hours honing a blade by scraping it on concrete.

I heard one story about a shank designed from a coat hanger and used with surgical precision. Three inmates, walking around the prison yard, approached a man leaning against a wall, paused only briefly, and left as the man slid down the wall dead. The killer knew exactly where to insert the hangar below his ribs, shoving it up into the victim's heart.

Sometimes, brute force did the job. Three months into my stay, a man was killed while pumping iron. He was working out in the gym when somebody slammed a heavy steel plate into his head. Several inmates were nearby, but nobody saw anything. It was just another unsolved prison murder.

Whether it was to preserve my good time or my own life, I could not afford the luxury of unleashing the anger or martial arts skills I had so easily wielded in the nightclubs and streets of the free world. When challenged by troublemakers, I had to be disciplined.

Otherwise, Sergio said, I'd only be taking their bait.

In the first few days in Manchester, I noticed how people brought Ciccio food and treated him with great respect in the chow hall. During one meal, he offered me fruit to take to my cell.

I declined, knowing it was against the rules to take it back to my unit. But Ciccio would walk right out with his, and the guards wouldn't say a word. Sergio did the same thing. I was intrigued by how they could do this, but I didn't ask why they had such privileges.

After a few days, Ciccio told me about his family, showing pictures, some of them set in New York. He told me he owned pizza restaurants.

"Ciccio, why are you here?" I finally asked.

He smiled. "They accused me of being a part of an organization and took me down."

"What kind of organization?" I asked.

"Oh, you know, Italian."

"Well, you probably have heard of the Pavonés," I said, jokingly.

"Pavoné? No I haven't."

Then I said, "Detroit."

He named families he knew in Detroit. I recognized some of the names. They'd made the headlines in the Detroit papers in years past.

Later that evening, an inmate ran down to our unit and poked his head into Ciccio's door.

"Hey, Ciccio, you're on TV," he said, excitedly. "Come on."

I followed Ciccio to the day room to watch. TV newsman Geraldo Rivera was airing a special, showing the hierarchy of the Mafia.

Prisoners were saying, "Look, Ciccio, that's you."

I teased him. "What do they mean, that's you? That guy is young and handsome." I thought everyone was joking.

Then the television screen showed a close-up. Indeed, it was the man sitting next to me. He was *Francesco "Ciccio" Barzino*, a boss in a major New York crime family. The title boss, or "don" as we called him, was only given to men who'd earned great respect.

I lost my breath. "Mr. Barzino, I apologize," I said. "I had no idea."

He laughed. "See, I told you I'm big. I'm a boss."

He slapped me on the back and added, "Come on, Pavoné, take it easy."

Sergio told me, "Don't let him scare you. He's a good guy."

To this day, I do not know what crimes Ciccio committed. However, he was aware of the charges that landed me in prison very soon after my arrival. I assumed he had me checked out to see if I was an informant. I didn't want to be a snitch. I just wanted to do my time and get on with my life. I also knew all the other inmates, except Sergio, were intimidated by his presence.

I decided I'd just be myself with him and that included teasing him.

He liked to wear long underwear and I'd tease him about being "sexy."

He'd pull up his pant leg, showing his thermals around the prison, saying, "I'm sexy, yeah."

I was on the phone with my mother once when he walked by.

"What's your mother's name?" he asked.

"Gloria."

He thought I said *lawyer*. "Good lawyer? I need a good lawyer, I'm in for 35 years!"

After Sergio translated what I really said, Ciccio motioned for the phone. I handed it to him. He told my mother he was watching out for me. And he did.

Soon, he was telling other inmates I was his "nephew." He shortened "Bernadino" to "Dino," a nickname that would stick for my entire term. Prison officials assigned Sergio as my cellmate.

Even so, I still had to look after myself on more than one occasion. Once, an inmate and I were walking down a corridor when a prisoner approached tightly gripping a mop.

He glared at the inmate I was with, saying, "You stepped on my floor, man." He started to lift the mop to hit him.

I grabbed the handle. "Hey, it's okay," I said.

His anger instantly turned toward me. He made verbal threats and a crowd quickly gathered, sensing they would soon see some action. I was confident in my martial arts skills, but I also knew self-defense in prison was counterproductive. I didn't want an altercation on my record.

I tried a little psychology. "You're doing a lot of talking," I said. "And you're talking because you're scared."

"Scared?"

"Yeah, anyone who talks is scared to make his move."

He inched forward. I went into a karate stance.

He blinked. "What are you — trained?" he asked.

"Come and find out," I said.

He glared at me for a few more seconds. Finally, he turned and walked away.

I considered myself fortunate, and my good fortune in the daily challenges of prison life continued. Few wanted to challenge Ciccio Barzino by harming one of his friends. His celebrity status alone carried clout.

At times, interacting with him reminded me of humorous scenes I'd seen in films like Martin Scorcese's "Good Fellas."

Food was a precious commodity in Manchester, and I had problems with the prison diet. Almost everything was cooked in butter or oil, which for years have caused cramps in my digestive track. I approached the prison officials about getting a special diet, but they ignored my requests.

Then one day a physician's assistant pulled me aside.

"Pavoné, you're Mr. Barzino's nephew, aren't you?" he asked.

"I only know him from here," I said.

"He told me you're his nephew."

I chuckled.

"Meet me in the back of the hospital," the assistant said. "I'll arrange a special pass for you."

When I arrived later, he had a special request. He wanted me to get Barzino's autograph. "Not for me," he said. "It's for my brother."

"I can do that," I said, "but in return, maybe you can help me. Ciccio needs medication for his gout and I'm allergic to oil and butter and everything here is soaked with the stuff. So I need a special diet."

"Did you try to get these through the proper channel?"

"I went through the official bureaucracy. They said, 'This is a prison, not a health spa.'"

"Yeah, they always say clever things like that."

"I don't get it," I continued. "The Hindus get special meals and so do the Muslims. Why can't those of us who have allergies get special diets?"

I told him I'd get Ciccio Barzino's autograph whether he could accommodate me or not. The next day Ciccio received his medicine and I got my "special diet." I was allowed to stand in the kitchen and run boiling water over my food until all the oils were rinsed off.

As I indicated, food was not allowed in the cells, but that didn't stop Ciccio and Sergio. They even cooked it in their cells. Tomato sauces, vegetables, garlic and other ingredients would show up in Ciccio's room. We cooked pasta dishes using an electrical cord attached to a makeshift hot plate, called a "stinger" in prison language.

The guards never said a word.

Prison officials learned I had a college degree and had attended Spanish classes in high school. Officially, they asked me to teach English as a second language to inmates. But when I reported to the director of the department, he told me that my assignment was to sit with Ciccio and entertain him.

I asked what I should do specifically.

The director said, "Read the paper, watch videos. Do whatever he wants. He likes to be with you and enjoys hanging out and talking to you. So that's your job here."

It all came to an end unexpectedly. I was in Manchester six months when my counselor called me to his office.

"There's been a mistake," he said.

"What kind of mistake?"

"You're not supposed to be here," he said. "You were supposed to be assigned to the minimum security camp when you got here."

"I already knew that," I said. "I've been saying that. I told you that, but it didn't happen."

The counselor told me I was going to be transferred to Morgantown, West Virginia. "It will be better for you there," he added. "And you'll be closer to your family."

One inmate, however, apparently had other plans for my future.

A few days later, the night before I left Manchester, Ciccio wanted

Sergio and me to watch TV with him in an activity room. We'd taken our seats, when suddenly a Jamaican prisoner became furious, claiming I was sitting in what he had decided was his chair. He told me so in the usual direct terms commonly used in prison.

"Okay," I said. I got up.

Ciccio grabbed my arm and said, "Sit down." He turned to the Jamaican and said, "Grab a chair over there."

The inmate obeyed.

I didn't hear another word from him that night until later, when he showed up in my room brandishing a blade. I was sitting, making some notes about a business idea for the future.

"Dino, what you did was wrong," he said. "Now I got to slice you."

The career criminals always talked that way. They acted as if some outside force compelled them to violence. But I knew his real motivation. He wanted to start a fight so I'd lose my good time and be stuck in Manchester for the rest of my sentence.

I reached for my shoes and covered my hands with them — a self-defense move for a knife attack, something I'd learned from Master Sam Santilli and Master Willie Adams. Then I jumped up, bracing my back against the wall. I did all this faster than it takes to talk about it.

I looked him in the eyes and said calmly, "Close the door so the guards can't hear you scream."

He looked surprised by how fast I had put myself into position to defend against his blade. He also could see that I wasn't afraid.

Moments later, he walked out of my cell.

I went to Ciccio's cell and told him what had happened.

"I'll take care of it, Dino."

Within five minutes, guards escorted the Jamaican out of our cell block. Ciccio put the word out I was to be left alone until my transfer or they would have to deal with him.

Later, before the lights went out, I said goodbye to both Ciccio and Sergio. We kissed one another on the cheeks, an Italian formality.

"I'm going to miss you," Ciccio said. "I love you in my heart." There were many tears.

I was grateful for their friendship. Neither asked for anything in return. I simply treated both men as I would have wanted to be treated, and they never gave me a reason to treat them otherwise.

I'm not sure how I would have fared in Manchester without Sergio and Ciccio. Certainly, the education and the security they provided allowed me to concentrate on other more important matters. One of them was preparing to put my life back together for the day I got out. That included the conception and design of a new business — one I was sure could help people who wanted to make a new start in life.

Through the many nights in my cell, I'd already begun the job.

CHAPTER 14

~

MUD AND STARS

An anonymously authored poem, popular in prison, goes:

Two men looked out
from prison bars.
One saw mud
the other saw stars.

Some see mud. Some see stars. I believe what we decide to "see" is our choice, and also where we'll go with that vision every day of our lives.

I remember looking out from my prison window and knowing absolutely what I'd do when I was released — not only with my work, but with the way I'd look at life.

For me, prison brought clarity. I saw that the attitudes of people in prison were simply amplified versions of the kind of thinking that keeps people on the outside from realizing a rewarding life. In prison, people feel sorry for themselves. In prison, most inmates assign fault: They took the fall for a buddy. They were set up. Their lawyer sold them out. They're all innocent. They're not responsible for their crimes. They're not responsible for their sentences.

Somebody else is.

Is it any different than the lies we tell ourselves on the outside? *I am not responsible for my life. Somebody else is.* Blaming someone else is seductive. It gets us in the habit of thinking that what others do — or don't do — drives the forces that define our existence.

It's a simple, but profound truth that came to me: If I don't take responsibility for my actions, I put others in charge of my life. Then I live in a prison of my own making — one that I can't leave. Incarceration, I decided, was not defined by razor wire and insurmountable brick walls.

It was determined by my heart and mind.

It had to begin with me, and then I had to reach out. Knowing right from wrong was not enough. I also had to accept the fact that I didn't have all the answers. Sometimes I needed to reach out for help from family and trusted friends. Sometimes I had to reach out to God to help me do the right thing. I had to cultivate humility.

Humility is an important part of personal growth.

That's what my family's longtime trusted friend Jerry O'Connor liked to say. He learned that in AA. When we're open to learn new ideas, that's when great visions and opportunities appear.

Sometimes, they were right in front of us all along.

My vision was realized during a visit by my mother at FCI Manchester. She faithfully made the seven-hour trip every other weekend. She also wrote frequently as did my sister, my father and step-mom. Master Santilli and Master Rick and Connie Ballard and Jerry O'Connor and his wife, Marie, all wrote. Many people wrote. Family and friends became my teachers.

"Bernie," my mother said. "I think we're going to need to get some office space. They're too many people coming to the house."

"For what?" I asked.

Credit counseling and credit repair, she said. What started as a part-time service for family and friends was generating word-of-mouth referrals.

She added, "I know there is a really good business here."

In the following weeks, she was able to rent a small office in Livonia, a Detroit suburb. It was a modest beginning. The office was in one room with two desks, one for my mother, the other for my fiancée, Tina, whom my mother trained in the business.

The service, Credit Counselors of Michigan, advertised in area newspapers. From repairing my own credit in 1988 and watching my mother work with friends and relatives in our house, I knew it would be a tough business to tackle on a larger scale.

Like many financial services, credit reporting has evolved into a multi-headed behemoth in the information age. Some rudimentary system of credit appraisal must have developed during the Renaissance simultaneously with the origin of modern banking in Italy around 1400 A.D. Most likely it involved word-of-mouth and a few notes kept in files. In America, formal methods of credit reporting go back at least to the middle of the nineteenth century. That's when Dunn and Bradstreet emerged as the leading source of credit information in the United States. But D&B only reported on businesses.

In the days before credit cards, little demand existed for credit reports on individuals, and the labor-intensive methods for assembling and selling the information made it impractical to keep track of millions of consumers. More than a century passed before consumer credit began expanding rapidly in the 1950s. Along with that expansion came an urgent need for credit reports on people. Several companies rushed to fill the need, and the most successful of them became large, highly-profitable corporations. Along with size came bureaucratic arrogance. Eventually the abuses became so great that Congress passed the Fair Credit Reporting Act in 1970.

That law dictates in great detail how information must be reported by lenders, how it's kept by the credit reporting agencies, and how consumers can correct faulty information. But monitoring the information presented a time-consuming challenge. Credit reports had to be obtained from not one, but all three of the major credit reporting agencies that track payment histories of consumers. Incorrectly entered data had to be challenged with letters. There was substantial follow-up involved to see if flawed entries were removed as required by law.

I knew my mother would be mired deep in paperwork, and I was stuck in a prison cell for two years. But I reflected: If reporting agencies could use computers to enter information, why couldn't we use computers to check data? Why couldn't I design a program that could check all their entries on reports, determining if they complied with the law? Such a program would have to be designed to work on legally generated reports requested by consumers, as was their right under the law. I knew I wouldn't be able to hack into the systems of the credit agencies. I didn't want to. That would be illegal.

The problem was I knew nothing about computer programming. However, a number of inmates did at FCI Manchester, those with professional and business backgrounds. I asked a lot of questions.

"You don't need to know about programming," one told me. "You need to design a flow chart."

"And a flow chart does what?"

"It's the tasks what you want the software to accomplish. You hire a programmer to put the chart into computer language. But first you have to get all the tasks organized on paper, map it all out, so the programmer knows what you want the computer to do."

The possibilities kindled my imagination. I jotted down ideas in my room every night. I kept it simple at first. I thought: The mapping process doesn't have to be advanced, just straightforward. But once I established a structure, more possibilities appeared. I designed options and provisions for more complex searches.

Pages of notes piled up in my cell.

I found myself getting more organized. I had a daily planner in prison and organized my activities and thoughts. I disciplined my time during the day and worked on the flow chart at night. I worked every night, sometimes until five in the morning. I found strength in the clarity of knowing what I was going to do with the rest of my life. I was going to put my program on a computer disk that would revolutionize the way we fix credit problems.

As I was designing the flow chart, I found myself questioning aspects of my life I hadn't previously considered. What had happened to the happy kid I had been? How did my life go so bad? Where did I go wrong? How can I stop other people from going down that path? How can I give others the new opportunities I was given before they got into trouble?

Perhaps I could build a business that would not only offer financial opportunities, but maybe, I decided, it could be the kind of enterprise that could draw on the hard lessons of my own life.

CHAPTER 15

THE TESTS OF TIME

When I was transferred from Manchester, I was optimistic. I figured the next facility would no doubt be cleaner and safer than the medium high-security prison I left. I was headed to Atlanta first. It was a 13-hour bus ride, with everyone packed into the seats and shackled, an armed guard sitting in the back.

My bus was filled with maximum-security lifers headed for the Atlanta Penitentiary. They were desperate men who would risk anything for a brief taste of freedom, or just for a scrap of senseless revenge. A dull hatred emanated from their sleepy eyes. They would be going from one dismal cell to another for years. Inmates called such transfers "diesel therapy." Prison administrators had good reasons for moving some prisoners around. Corrections administrators knew if certain inmates stayed too long in one place, they would use terror to organize private armies. To maintain their power they run rackets and have their thugs beat up or kill anyone who resists. When these shot-callers were transferred to a new prison, they would have no army to protect them so they would be in danger themselves. The armies they left behind were less trouble — at least until another ruthless criminal took them over.

I'd thought Manchester was bad, but Atlanta, where I would be held for two weeks, was hell on earth. The prison population was nearly 2,000. Toiletries like shampoo and bar soap often weren't available, but the place was awash with drugs and homemade liquor. Murderers served the long chow line. Violent criminals had access to you, particularly when you were housed in a big open holding area as I was. It was a huge, fearsome prison. I felt like a character in a mob movie.

I tried to remain positive, but I slept little. I feared for my life.

After two weeks, authorities told me I'd be transferred by "Con Air" to the minimum security camp. Every major airport has its hangar for federal aviation. Unmarked airplanes, with a small American flag painted on the side, come and go from the hangars carrying federal prisoners. When the time came, we boarded such a plane in our prison jumpsuits. I'd been letting my hair grow since my incarceration and it had reached shoulder length. Before I left Atlanta, I'd put Vaseline in my hair, trying to condition it after two weeks of washing it with bar soap.

A federal agent sitting across from me in a jumper seat asked how I landed in the federal system.

"I got caught," I said.

"No, what did you do?" she asked.

"Something really stupid," I said. "It wasn't violent."

She touched my face and told me, "You're beautiful. Wish I had a chance to see you on the outside."

"Get me out of here," I joked.

"I wish I could."

That's the closest I ever got to a female who had any interest in me while I was behind bars. It was reassuring, however, that my fiancée, Tina, was waiting for me at home. But back at Manchester, Sergio had warned me that 90 percent of the relationships men had before going to prison don't last six months. But I was not concerned because Tina was not only working with my mother in Credit Counselors of Michigan, she'd moved into the family home.

We landed in Lewisburg, Pennsylvania, where I would be held temporarily at one of the federal penitentiaries inmates called "The Big House," an ironic nickname given my fond memories of the Safie "Big House." Though it held only 1,000 inmates, it was full of mournful noises, rows of steel doors grinding and the shuffle of aimless feet on concrete. At other times an oppressive silence settled over the place, sometimes broken by nerve-shattering screams.

Even in that environment, I could feel my confidence growing, the payoff from the work on the flow chart in previous months. I hadn't felt that way since I worked on the nightclub project. I decided to put the organizational skills I knew I once had with people on the outside to the test inside prison walls. After arriving at Lewisburg, I realized that the inmates were abusing the phone system, which caused all kinds of arguments and disagreements over phone privileges. My problem was my diet. It was impossible to get food that didn't aggravate my allergies. I organized the telephone schedule in my cell block, assigning times to my fellow prisoners. Inmates could trade their times with others and I took the vacant slots, periodically bartering those for food. Forty men joined the arrangement.

I received the food I needed and the arguing and fighting stopped.

On December 20, 1994, authorities transported me on another

bus to Morgantown, West Virginia. It would be my last stop in the federal prison system and just in time for a Christmas visit from Mom. Her visits now were far happier for both of us because I was over the hump. I was more than halfway through my sentence.

Morgantown had a beautiful church and grounds, tennis courts, and a putting green. I'd finally arrived at the kind of federal "country club" prison so often derided in the media. But behind the scenes, many of its 1,000 inmates still staked out turf and assaults took place. One inmate was beaten into a coma while I was there.

Prison, any prison, is a dangerous place.

I became an altar boy. My duty was to ring the bell during key points in the Mass. Once I forgot the bell. Desperate situations call for desperate measures, so I used my voice to give my best imitation of a bell ringing.

The priest stopped the mass. "Dino, what's wrong with you? Are you okay?"

Kiddingly, I assured him that I was all right. He went on with the ceremony. I never forgot the bell again.

I could feel myself healing — mentally, physically and spiritually. I felt connected with God in Morgantown. I said the rosary every day. I prayed daily for guidance and help. I got a job in the card shop right next to the sanctuary in the chapel. For exercise, I had worked out with weights and sometimes walked 10 miles a day in Manchester and I continued exercising at Morgantown. I decided that if it was important to do all these things to survive prison, they would have to be the routines I must do on the outside to be remain focused.

I learned a wealth of good habits in prison.

My continual challenge remained finding fat-free food, a quest which landed me in a little trouble with the prison priest. As an altar boy, I thought the holy wafers were unconsecrated if they were still in the bag he used to bring them to the altar. I began munching on them after Mass.

One day he caught me.

"Dino, how can you do that?" he asked, his eyebrows furrowed. "You know those are holy wafers — *consecrated* holy wafers."

"Father, they're still in the bag," I said. "How can they be blessed?"

"The blessing goes through anything."

Explaining my dietary problems, I said, "The wafers are fat-free."

"Dino, no more. You can't eat the wafers, consecrated or not."

He looked at me for a few moments, then shook his head. "Dino, the unconsecrated ones are in the other cupboard," he said, smiling and pointing to the cabinet.

I ate bags and bags of those nutritious wafers at Morgantown.

My mother's visits continued. We spent our time discussing how the family was doing in Michigan and working on the details of the credit repair business, which was growing. With each visit I was increasingly optimistic about the flow chart for the credit repair program. I couldn't wait to get out and find a programmer to put it into computer language.

Not all the news she brought from home was good. My fiancée was miserable, she said, and always complaining. Then came the crusher. Tina was seeing another man.

I called her from prison. "I want you to keep the ring," I told her. "But you're going to have to leave my mother's house. It's time for you to go home."

Many nights I talked for hours with a friend at Morgantown. "I feel so frustrated," I told him. "I'm helpless in here but I try to work it out."

Yet, in time, even the loss of the woman I loved turned out to be a valuable lesson. In previous years, such emotional stress had compelled me to chase after the illusion of power through self-destructive behavior — whether it was seeking out bullies or speeding in my car or breaking the law.

In Morgantown, I found a simple truth: Sometimes the best thing to do is nothing. And with time, the bad feelings eventually pass.

I continued working on my flow chart every night. I was convinced the computer program was going to be a breakthrough piece of technology. I briefed my mother on my progress, but she didn't seem to realize the magnitude and depth I had reached with the mapping process.

Everything seemed to be working together for the good.

The anger management skills I'd learned as a result of my assault charges also were paying off. I'd walked away from many situations in prison that would have resulted in violence given the mind set I had years earlier. Instead, I'd accumulated "good time."

One day, I was summoned to the corrections counselor's office and given exhilarating news: I would be able to serve the last six months of my sentence at a halfway house in Detroit.

Prison authorities released me in September of 1995. My mother made the travel arrangements. I had asked her to give me a long layover at the airport because I wanted to shop, unwind, and adjust. I knew that once I reached Detroit I would have to report to the halfway house and my time again would no longer be my own.

I savored walking around the airport in Pittsburgh. I delighted in the simple realization that I was no longer wearing prison clothes.

I took a seat at a table in a TGI Friday's restaurant. I watched people and my surroundings for a long time. A young couple held hands. A mother fed her child. A large family organized its food order. People interacted without posturing. Their eyes were bright. Laughter punctuated conversations.

The air seemed saturated with freedom. I felt overwhelmed with gratitude.

I must have looked strange because the bartender came over.

"Are you okay?" he asked.

"I'm going to be fine, just fine," I said quietly.

"Can I get you a drink?"

"Iced tea."

He studied me carefully. "You sure I can't get you a real drink?"

"I don't like alcohol," I said. I wanted my senses sharp. I wanted to see and hear everything clearly.

A minute later, he brought the iced tea.

"Where did you just come in from?" he asked.

It was one of the rare times in my life that I had only a few words to say. I responded in the simplest of terms.

"I've been gone for awhile," I said. "And now I'm going home."

CHAPTER 16

A GESTURE OF TRUST

My mother picked me up at Detroit Metropolitan Airport and took me to the residence I would call home for the next six months. It was a one-story, converted community center in one of Detroit's toughest neighborhoods on the near east side. Some 50 other parolees lived there, sharing rooms and common bathrooms. I would have to sign in and out and be back at 7 p.m. every day.

Everyone calls them "halfway houses" — but they are definitely the better half. They are better because there are no bars on the windows. They are better because the pervasive fear, anger and skepticism found in prison loosen their grip. Some former inmates, however, never make the transition psychologically. They carry the mistrust and posturing developed behind bars into the outside world, and their work and personal relationships suffer as a result.

I was halfway to sweet freedom, I told myself. I immediately poured my energy into the credit repair concept I'd worked on in prison. An old friend, Chuck Shattelroe, owner of Metro-Power Sports, North America's number one Honda motorcycle dealership, had a job waiting for me. This helped me fulfill my parole requirements. He gave me the opportunity to work in sales, but also the flex time to pursue my own dream. I will always be grateful to him for that. Most men coming out of prison struggle to find a decent job, let alone one with such latitude.

My mother picked me up every morning for work and took me back to the halfway house each night. Ideas streamed out of my mind on our daily drives. I wanted to start formalizing our plans for the new business.

My mother later told a friend, "When Bernie was released he hit the ground running. We said, 'slow down, not so fast.' But there was no stopping him. I had no idea how much he'd already worked out in his mind all those months he was away."

Soon, I was also bending Theresa's ear. Theresa was working as a regional manager for the same chain of hair salons that had employed my mother. I told her my vision went well beyond the little office of Credit Counselors of Michigan. I planned to expand to a couple of other major cities, like New York and Chicago.

I was back hardly three weeks when Theresa called me. "Bernie, I want you to come to my house for dinner," she said. "I have someone for you to meet."

His name was Abood Samaan, she said. Theresa was working with him for a national salon chain. She'd known him when she was in college and they'd renewed their friendship after bumping into each other in Las Vegas. He came from a respected Palestinian family.

"I was telling him about some of your ideas," Theresa said. "He has some experience. He's looking to get into a new venture."

I figured, why not? Maybe he had something to offer. The very least I could do was break bread with the man.

When we met, I was struck immediately how different our

personalities were. He had penetrating eyes and a stillness about him that many people might find unnerving. I wear my heart on my sleeve. I'm animated and quick to speak. What you see is what you get. I might have thought Abood was shy, if it were not for the deliberateness in the way he moved and spoke.

I vaguely sketched out some of my ideas over dinner. He ate quietly, asking only a few basic questions. He was an exceptional listener. I decided to stop talking entirely, letting some silence fall between us.

Finally, he looked at me calmly and said, "You say you want to go to New York and Chicago with this credit repair service, what about the rest of the country?"

"We could do that," I said.

I excused myself from the table for a moment and sought out my sister in the kitchen. "What are you doing?" I asked her quietly. "Here we go with investors again. I've been through this before with the nightclub. I can't take any more insincere people. I need people around me who understand what I'm trying to do."

"Does Abood strike you as insincere?"

I thought about it. The "investors" in my past were always talking, and delivering nothing. Abood had said little, but what did that mean? Maybe the man was simply void of hype. Maybe that was good.

Theresa said, "Bernie, look at me. Abood's family owns 22 hotels. He's very serious and he's very capable of doing this. So get back in there."

She was right. I don't know if it was the nightclub experience or those months in prison. Maybe it was a combination of both, but I found it hard to trust anyone. I had to push through that if I was going to do business in the world.

I went back to the dinner table and opened up a little. It was difficult. But as I talked, I saw something glisten and it caught my eye. It was Abood's watch, catching a reflection from the dining room light.

"Man, that's a beautiful watch," I said.

He took it off and handed it to me across the table. "Try it on," he said.

I slipped it on my wrist. "Where is it from?" I asked.

"The royal family of Qatar." Qatar was an independent emirate on the Persian Gulf, he said. "It was a gift."

I admired it for a moment. I slipped it off and handed it back.

"Keep it," Abood said.

"Would you stop?" I said, laughing at the idea.

"No, you like it. It's yours."

I slipped it back on my wrist. I still have the watch.

I leaned forward across the table. "I don't know if you know this," I said. "But I just got out of prison."

He didn't even blink. "It must have been hell," he said. "But I'm not interested in any of that. I want to know more about this company. And like I asked, how are we going to market this and take it across the country?"

Abood had no ulterior motives. I could feel it that night at the dinner table. In fact, he had ideas. He'd had some experience with network marketing — the direct selling of a service or product through the word of mouth between family, friends and associates.

I told him I'd been doing some research. My flow charts were completed for the credit repair program. I'd been told by knowledgeable people that once my system was translated into computer language, it could be worth as much as $300,000. But we needed operating capital. We needed staff, equipment and office space.

"We're talking about a major investment," I said.

"How major?"

"A good $750,000 or so," I said.

Abood looked me in the eyes and said, "That would not be a problem." I still had some reservations, not about the man sitting across from me, but about keeping my own promises. I was honest with Abood. There were other people I wanted to bring aboard.

"A long time ago I promised a cousin of mine that we'd always give each other opportunities in business," I said. I was thinking of Stevie Safie. "I'd like to take this concept to him as well. I also want to call my Honda dealership employer and old friend Chuck Shattelroe and offer him the opportunity, too."

Abood understood.

Later, Abood told a mutual friend what was going through his mind during our first meeting:

"I consider myself to be a common sense person and pretty streetwise. But I'm not the type to just look at him getting out of prison as a reason to shy away. I tend to look at the positive part of people. Common sense told me that we could have something great here. I had no experience in the credit industry. However, friends of mine had gone into business and things had not gone as well as they had hoped. This left them with less than perfect credit. So I knew it didn't mean someone was rotten to the core just because their credit report had some marks on it."

But Abood would have to wait.

The next week, I made my pitch to both Chuck and Stevie. Chuck wanted to concentrate on his own business. Stevie kept asking for more information and wanted to see hard numbers. He had a successful basement waterproofing business. It became clear to me that only Abood and my mother seemed to understand what I had in mind.

Frankly, in retrospect, I'm not sure I really understood what I had in mind. I only knew that I was on to something that had no limits. With the avalanche of credit card offers being sent in the mail to everyone from high school graduates to established consumers, I knew millions of Americans were facing credit problems, and the numbers were increasing daily. And the only way to meet their needs on a large scale was a service that could employ the speed, efficiency and thoroughness of computer technology.

Abood, I later learned, was thinking along the same lines.

"Knowing what little I knew — except for the key fact that a lot of people need credit repair — I was intrigued by Bernie's computer search program," Abood later told a friend. "Here we had a potential industry of almost unlimited size. I had some knowledge of network marketing concepts from being in a business as an independent representative. Gloria brought years of business experience, and Bernie was focused and driven. A huge market was out there. If we could roll out a hard-hitting program and put together a business, we might have something phenomenal."

A couple of weeks after our first meeting, Abood and I met at the house in Plymouth and worked out a partnership investment. I tore a yellow legal pad in half and suggested that we each write down what we wanted out of the deal.

As Abood made notes, I stared at his writing.

He looked up and smiled. "Are we taking a test?"

I smiled back. Something felt right about this man.

We gave each other our notes when we finished. It didn't surprise me that we easily agreed on a deal. I suggested taking both pieces to an attorney to have a formal agreement drawn up.

"Would you like to use your attorney for the first draft?" I asked.

"No, yours will be fine," he said.

My attorney came back in a week with a thick document that formalized our partnership. Abood read through it once with me. We decided he could forward copies to our respective attorneys for any suggested changes. I followed him to his car and saw him put the document in the back seat. He folded it and shoved it between the seat and the back cushion.

A couple days later he handed me with the same document. I saw him pull it from the same place he'd put it in the car. It was obvious he'd never given it to his lawyer.

"Where are your attorney's changes?" I asked anyway.

"No changes," Abood said.

I laughed. "What do you mean, no changes? Attorneys are paid to make changes; it's their meal ticket."

"Well, I don't have any changes," Abood said.

He signed the agreement and handed it to me.

It was a profound moment for me. Obviously, his attorney had never even seen the agreement. That kind of trust warmed me deeply. In time, I would discover a man with one of the kindest spirits I know. He reminded me in many ways of my father. His trust and generosity would surpass anything I've ever experienced outside my closest family.

But that night, I lectured him. "Are you crazy to be so trusting? I could have taken your money and left the country. I could have gone on vacation."

"I know you're not going anywhere," Abood said.

He was right. I was still in the halfway house, but that really had nothing to do with it. Abood, I decided, was family.

He's been family ever since.

CHAPTER 17

BOOTING UP

Hundreds of hours had gone into design of the credit repair process that my mother, Abood and I believed would form the bedrock of our new company. My raw notes were trade secrets in the making. I couldn't turn over the design of the program to just anyone.

In November of 1995, only a few weeks after meeting Abood, I stopped by a restaurant near the Honda motorcycle dealership where I was working and looked up from the menu to see a face I hadn't seen in more than two years.

"Todd," I shouted.

Soon, we were embracing.

Todd Renzi and I had first met through a mutual friend in 1988 at a local gym. He was the kind of person I've always been drawn to — full of ideas, self-motivated and blessed with a kind spirit.

"Man, where have you been?" Todd asked.

Prison, I answered. I told him the whole story.

"And what about you?" I asked. "I'm sure you haven't been dealing with the law."

Ironically, he had but he'd been very productive. Todd had his own consulting firm called The Renzi Group. It specialized in technical support and consulting for police agencies and Michigan courts. The firm had developed the process for communications between police cars and governmental entities. Among his many talents, Todd Renzi was a computer programmer.

"Todd, I've got this idea," I began. "But I'm having problems. I'm not sure what computer language to use. And I'm not sure who I can trust."

As it turned out, I could trust him.

Less than a week later, we signed a confidentiality agreement, establishing the program as a trade secret. But legal paperwork is only as valid as the good faith behind it. Stolen technology and plagiarism are the bane of many businesses. Legal agreements often simply set up the rules for costly lawsuits which can drain firms of energy and funds.

I never worried about that with Todd.

We met regularly, starting the process of turning my notes into software. It had to be designed to accept and process numerous categories of data. Our customers would obtain their credit reports, send them to us and then we would punch the information into our program, which would automate the entire process. That was the power of the program. It had never been done before.

Many months later, Todd would look back on those months as a major challenge. Reflecting on the task, he told me: "I began by playing with the computer concept. But it wasn't something where I could sit down and work on an hour today and another hour tomorrow. I needed to pack in ten-to-twelve-hour sessions with complete focus to get the idea in place. It took me many months of intense concentration, hard slugging and long hours to produce a testing model of the program."

There would be many more weeks of testing the prototype, working out the bugs and finding more efficient ways to process the data.

Todd's work was impressive — especially considering he was doing the work for free. But Todd, like Abood and my mother, believed in my vision. I was so grateful for his trust as well as his effort, I assigned him a percentage of ownership of the program and he's also a top corporate officer in our company. The computer disk he designed and has continued to improve over the years is locked in a safe today — for good reason. An independent appraisal in 2001 valued it as high as $247 million.

That kind of value, however, was beyond the reach of my own imagination as the holiday season came in late 1995. I was still dealing with the requirements of the halfway house with its three levels of supervision. If you behaved and met all the restrictions, the authorities lessened the supervision and your time gradually became your own.

I signed in and out with great care and met all the deadlines. I also was respectful not only to my supervisors, but other parolees as well.

I wanted to be free of the criminal justice system forever.

The restrictions meant Abood and I could meet only during my limited free time. More than a few business meetings ended with the words, "I've got to get back and sign in." We'd get together for dinner after I finished work at the car dealership. We met during weekends when I was given passes to my mother's home. We largely worked on concepts at first. I did not have enough free time to devote to detail work. With the repair program expected to be ready for use in mid-1996, much more remained to be accomplished. Todd Renzi was designing the program to serve more than 100,000 customers. We needed clients, lots of clients, to realize its full potential.

The heavy lifting began four months after parole officials released me from the halfway house and permitted me to live at home with my mother. I was still under the supervision of a parole officer, but my time was largely my own.

Abood responded by moving in — quite literally. Having all three of us in the same house saved a lot of time. Work began over morning coffee, continued through lunch and dinner, and often extended late into the night.

We discovered a chemistry in the combination of three diverse personalities: I was on fire with ideas and adventurous concepts; my mother was the no-nonsense, straight-talking negotiator, undeterred by obstacles; Abood was the analytical voice of reason, always conscious of the financial bottom line.

As Abood later put it, "I didn't major in business in college and neither had Gloria. This was not a serious problem. Courses in entrepreneurship are rare or unknown. Knowing how to deal with people, and having the common sense to resolve problems and find solutions immediately were our strengths. And the three of us were the perfect mix. When one came in negative, the other two came in positive, and we balanced each other out."

It's a combination that continues.

But back then, I was so focused on our new enterprise, I put my own appearance on hold. I hadn't cut my hair since entering prison. There seemed to be something significant about the hair that now fell past my shoulders. It represented time served, and my climb back from near self-destruction. I told myself that perhaps I would cut it when I felt I'd fully atoned for my past.

Plus, I told myself I didn't have time to contemplate a haircut. We had an enormous amount of work to do as quickly as possible. It was amazing how many different things have to be done to operate any interstate business efficiently and in full compliance with federal and state laws, and local ordinances. We were entering a highly regulated business.

I would walk around the living room, talking out loud. "We need attorneys, accountants, telephones, printing, marketing, computers, construction, banking, financial consultants, office design, leasing, insurance, and bonds," I'd say. "We need to register the company nationally. We're going to need staff. We're going to need a staff structure."

I reached out. I called a friend who was the founder of another major network marketing company and asked for advice. He educated me in the basics of network marketing organizations. I called other friends for recommendations on everything from top attorneys to office furniture.

Our promotional materials had a humble beginning. I designed a company logo myself at my mother's desk, then went to a national printing franchise popular with college students and small businesses to refine it. Finally, I took it to a graphic artist.

The busy designer tried to put me off.

"Look, we need this now," I said.

It cost a little extra, but we got it quickly.

Don't procrastinate, I told myself — and anyone else who would listen. Avoid the accumulation of distractive busywork. Such mental baggage stifles the imagination and limits the focus on the tasks ahead.

"Do it now!" It became a personal philosophy as well as a company credo.

We had to have the logo quickly because, in the house in Plymouth, we not only had devised a marketing plan, we'd written our own sales and training literature. The logo was going to go on our first sales package — a relatively simple binder with the phrase, "Let Your Future Begin" on the cover.

As it turned out, there were two good reasons Abood's belief in the potential of network marketing had won the day in our long discussions. When I first conceived a national credit repair company using the new software, I was leaning toward franchising. I imagined thousands of stores where consumers could go for our services. By comparison, network marketing utilizes independent representatives and pays a commission to representatives producing sales. It also pays them to build a business by recruiting other reps. However, whatever approach we adopted, we faced a couple of major obstacles.

First was the poor reputation of the credit repair industry itself. Some of that reputation had been earned by unscrupulous operators who took consumers' money and failed to live up to promises that included everything from removing credit histories to creating new credit identities. Unethical companies used the Internet to exploit consumers. The Federal Trade Commission and state attorney generals were issuing warning bulletins about credit repair companies. Credit reporting agencies sent letters to credit repair clients, warning that many companies were "deceiving customers," a practice that continues today. The credit reporting agencies, financial institutions and news media exploited the horror stories. There seemed to be a predictable cycle of press coverage. Near the end of the year, news organizations would publish reports urging consumers to check their credit reports for false and inaccurate information. Then, at the first of the year, stories would appear about credit repair scams. With the news media, the government and the credit reporting agencies all bashing the industry, the notion of a start-up company in credit repair trying to go national seemed daunting at the very least.

The second obstacle was the stigma of being denied credit. Someone's credit rating is very *personal.* A bad credit rating isn't likely to be discussed among casual company. For many, it ranks right alongside relationship problems, sexual proclivities and other closely held personal secrets. Even if bad ratings are not the fault of consumers, they will often believe that revealing a credit problem will reflect on their character and social status. The reports generated by the credit reporting agencies *are* powerful instruments. Inaccurate, erroneous and obsolete information routinely jeopardize people's ability to own homes, buy cars, rent apartments, or finance college educations. They can deny someone auto and life insurance and some employers even access them and the inaccurate information can cost people jobs.

Both the reputation of the industry and the subject matter itself demanded one element above all others in the marketing of our new company — *trust*. Network marketing was the solution. It represented the fastest way to move our new product.

As Abood put it, "Family, friends and close associates are going to listen to you, even trust you, more than they are from a toll-free number or from a stranger or from an advertisement. Those methods will get the interest of maybe one out of ten. But ten out of ten will listen when you hear it right from the mouth of someone you know."

It's a basic principle of network marketing — called the "warm market." These are potential customers with whom someone has already established rapport. A foundation of trust exists. Beyond the warm market is the "cold market," those people a sales representative doesn't know at all. But someone's cold market is also somebody else's warm one. So the way to reach it is to bring those people aboard, offering them incentives.

The services of the company, therefore, would be sold by word of mouth, one of the most powerful marketing forces in a free economy.

We spent many hours designing the initial plan, discussing such issues as: How much to charge customers; how much to charge people to become sales representatives; how we would reward them; and how the company hierarchy would be structured.

We wanted to design a company that didn't just pay people for recruiting other sales people. The company's products had to be sold. Otherwise, it was just a pyramid scheme.

First and foremost, we had a mission: We would provide services to people who needed them. We would keep our promises to both our customers and the people who sold our services.

It was all about trust. My personal moral beliefs aside, it had to be in order to thrive in an industry affected by scandal, controversy and privacy issues.

Our philosophy is reflected in our mission statement: "To exceed customer expectations by delivering the highest quality services possible and to create a peak performance atmosphere through which our independent representatives will develop their own opportunities to excel."

In February of 1996, in the heart of winter and five months after my release from prison, we were ready to launch our new company. We named it National Credit Repair.

But I wasn't quite ready to cut my hair.

CHAPTER 18

BUILDING THE FUTURE

About a hundred people showed up for the first public meeting to announce our new company in January of 1996. We held the business briefing in a presentation room on the seventh floor of the building in Livonia, a Detroit suburb, where National Credit Repair's small two-room suite was located. Abood displayed his usual calm competence and dignity. Beautifully coiffured and tailored, my mother was confident and witty. Sporting a suit, pony tail and earing, I took the floor and began the presentation.

"A few years ago I tried to open a nightclub and got into a little trouble," I began. "In fact, I got into quite a bit of trouble. Among other things, I lost $400,000."

I told my story and how I'd repaired my own credit profile with the credit reporting agencies in the late eighties.

The 45-minute presentation in some ways was not unlike the business briefing used by the company and our independent representatives. Millions of Americans were being denied loans, jobs and insurance. They were losing countless dollars on high interest rates because of inaccurate information on their credit reports. The creditors who supplied the data and bureaus that maintained this information were not following the guidelines of the Fair Credit Reporting Act. Consumers could correct and, thus, "repair" their reports.

"Is repairing your credit illegal or immoral?" I asked rhetorically. "Are we asking you to lie, or will we lie in order to repair credit? The answer to both of those questions is no. It is not only legal and moral to repair it, it is a right and obligation to do so."

Using a slide projector, I displayed Section 611 of the act which details the procedure for disputing and investigating inaccuracies. I read it: "If after such reinvestigation such information is found to be inaccurate or can no longer be verified, the consumer reporting agency shall promptly delete such information."

Many Americans had neither the time or resources to make sure their credit data was being reported and processed correctly, I told the audience. Correcting inaccuracies could be a complex and frustrating process. The system was unfair. Creditors and credit reporting agencies were holding consumers to rigid standards when it came to due dates, confusing grace periods and other fine print. But the agencies themselves were often ignoring the very guidelines Congress had enacted to protect the public.

Some of the abuses by the credit reporting industry were outrageous. I showed a video of a local news report about a suburban family who found out their credit reports were riddled with inaccurate information. When they tried to repair it themselves, they were largely ignored after spending weeks making phone calls and writing letters. The TV station put the credit reporting agency in its consumer "Hall of Shame".

I projected an Associated Press report from *The Detroit News.* The headline read: "Firm settles with FTC over credit reports." The story detailed how a credit reporting agency had failed to promptly delete inaccurate or unverified information from reports after consumers complained, and then failed to prevent the deleted information from reappearing.

"Studies show a high percentage of Americans have mistakes on their reports," I said. "We are launching National Credit Repair to an unlimited market. And it all begins right here."

We had one other service to offer: "Consumer Advantage," which is credit education, a more long-term service which helped consumers get their finances in order and maintain a positive credit rating. We were ready to sign up independent representatives to move our services and for them to build their own sales networks. For $99 they could become independent representatives and sell the credit repair service for $400 and receive commissions. If they signed up other representatives, they would received a percentage of their sales.

As I looked over the audience many were smiling. Most were friends and family members I'd urged to attend. Abood had invited his "warm market" as well. I'd love to be able to report that everyone rushed the lectern with pens to sign up. I'd love to be able to say that the company exploded out of the box.

It did not. We signed up a few folks, but I had a feeling they weren't really serious.

"I'm really happy for you, Bernie." I heard that a lot.

They were happy, I suspect, that I had turned my life around and had a new purpose, but they weren't quite ready to become part of the vision. They had their own careers and businesses.

I believe I'd made a great presentation, but I wasn't satisfied. I wanted reps — thousands of them. The day before the debut, we'd signed our first rep, our old family friend Jerry O'Connor.

Now we had a few more, but their hearts didn't seem to be in it.

One major issue facing us was the recruitment of many, many more reps. In the weeks ahead, Abood, my mother and I sold the concept of our company face to face, day and night. We scheduled weekly "opportunity briefings," as we called them, and recruited people to attend. We tried to prospect people in clubs, gyms, department stores, banks, boutiques and service stations. I made one-on-one presentations to people in their homes. I even tried to recruit a friend while standing up at his wedding.

Soon, those who signed up as reps began bringing their own recruits. It wasn't just my passion and enthusiasm that was swelling the numbers. Many of the new representatives were also using our credit repair service and seeing their ratings improve. They began giving glowing testimonials of the power of the National Credit Repair service. My presentation schedule grew from one meeting every Tuesday to five evening meetings a week. Our network of representatives began spreading to other states as new reps recruited distant friends and family.

We quickly outgrew our small office suite. We needed space and more staff to process the increasing volume of accounts. It took us three months to secure just a couple more rooms in the building where we were based.

I remember talking with Abood about the space dilemma. "Abood, we're going to need a whole wing of this building," I said.

We had to expand because, with the number of reps increasing, we could offer much more than Consumer Advantage and National Credit Repair to help people rebuild their lives. Many of the services I wanted to offer came out of my personal experience. I knew what it was like to be broke with creditors on my back, the phone company threatening to cut off service and institutions threatening to take legal action. Someone gave me a second chance. I wanted to give our customers the same breaks that were afforded to me. I wanted to help folks put their entire financial house in order, while at the same time giving them the opportunity to grow with our company as representatives.

In July of 1996, we changed our name to NCR Services. We made the change because in the next six months we would add our Financial Freedom Service, which could provide our customers with debt negotiation and reduction; Financial Lending Service, which would give them access to competitive mortgage rates; NCR Global Communications, which would offer long distance and Internet services at highly competitive rates; and NCR Legal Care, a nationwide legal service offered to representatives as an incentive.

My mother, Abood, and I believed we'd devised what we called "The Perfect Business" for our reps. It was ideal because it was accessible to anyone who was motivated to sell our services to a virtually unlimited marketplace. We had removed all the typical business impediments found in many network marketing enterprises. I remember listing them for our potential reps in our early literature:

- No expensive inventory.
- No shipments or deliveries.
- No collections.
- No customer risk.
- No payroll.

- No quotas.
- No merchandise to purchase.
- No confusing math or paperwork.
- No experience necessary.

By 1997, we were getting noticed. An offer came in over the transom from a broker. A credit reporting agency was prepared to offer us $10 million for our company. We would have to give the buyer our credit repair software and sign a non-compete contract.

"That's a lot of money," my mother said.

"The company is worth a lot more than ten million," I said. "Anyway, it's not for sale at any price."

Abood agreed.

It was an easy decision although we could have cashed out with more money than any one of us had ever banked in our lives. I could pay back the thousands in restitution I owed the federal court. I could pay back my family for the nightclub debacle.

I also knew many obstacles remained ahead, not to mention potential crises. There will always be crises in any ambitious endeavor. I'd learned that truth trying to launch the nightclub. People, money and promises I thought I could count on suddenly disappeared without warning. Often I was caught by surprise. Ultimately, it took me down. However, the nightclub experience also changed my way of planning for the future. It remains my modus operandi. You can't avoid a major problem beyond your control, but you can take away the element of surprise. I spend a lot of mental effort trying to anticipate worst-case scenarios. Some people may perceive that as negative thinking, but it's not. It's preparatory thinking. It's positive thinking. If you anticipate, you can utilize the resource of time. If you have time, you can prepare. And if you're prepared that means you have thought of other positive alternatives should your original plan fail as the result of forces beyond your control.

You're in control of your choices, not someone else.

We decided it was time to create a video. We hired a script writer and director. He started the project, but tragically contracted brain cancer and passed away.

"We'll do it ourselves," I announced.

We finished writing the script and hired a cameraman. We were shooting in Detroit when a police officer stopped to ask what we were doing.

"We're making a video," I said.

"What kind of video is it?" the uniformed officer asked.

"It's to help good people with bad credit," I told him.

The squad car blocked traffic for us.

Everywhere we went people responded positively to the idea of a company that fought for consumers' rights and financial stability in the complex world of credit finance.

Yet, I wasn't happy with our growth rate. We decided to take a hard look at our compensation structure for reps.

We had everything backwards, we decided. By offering independent representative positions at a low price we were actually working against our own cause. Some of our people were reluctant to sign up others as reps because that meant they were creating competition for their own commissions.

We decided to increase the representative fee from $99 to nearly $500. That would assure the reps were serious. Then we lowered the price of Consumer Advantage and National Credit Repair to make it easier for them to attract customers. Finally, we added incentives for reps to build their own sales organization. We called the incentives

Customer Acquisition Bonuses, or CABs. We would pay CABs to reps for assisting their newly sponsored representatives in making sales in a set time period. This allowed representatives to earn immediate income for developing their sales organization.

The reps responded enthusiastically. They began assisting other reps in making their presentations to customers and those interesting in joining the company's sales force. As co-founders of the company, we also made ourselves available to assist budding networks sprouting up in other cities.

Everyone was working together. We'd found the right combination to create a "family" where everyone shared in everyone else's success.

Suddenly, we were faced with dizzying growth. Our annual revenues skyrocketed 19,318 percent from 1995 to 1999.

Projecting my worst-case scenarios, I knew we had to be prepared for the day we might face a gold-plated crisis. The company could grow so fast it would collapse under its own weight. This could happen if cash flow lagged behind what would be needed to fund additional employees, equipment and facilities required to meet the increased volume.

That day came.

By September 1998, it was clear that our computer system would not be able to handle our rapidly increasing volume. We needed new, powerful and sophisticated software to keep track of our representatives and to compute their pay and incentives. Without it, we were headed for an accounting failure that would spread like an aggressive cancer and paralyze our corporation.

We were riding a tiger. Either we kept our seats or we'd fall off and get badly clawed or killed.

Abood, my mother and I sat down for a serious talk. Abood's

resources were already fully committed, as were mine. We needed to finance the purchase of the new software, but someone had to put up some collateral.

"You want a million-dollar home, fine cars, and a wonderful life?" I asked my mother. "That's where we're headed. But if we don't get this system, it's over."

My mother signed for the software herself, putting up the family house in Plymouth as collateral. It gave us the technology we needed to take us to the next benchmark.

By March of 1998, we were able to leave our cramped offices and move to our present corporate headquarters — in an emerald glass office building with easy access to the Detroit area freeway system. We also opened a distribution center in Los Angeles, and in 2001, moved our data processing operation to a new building in Canton Township, not far from our corporate headquarters.

The growing network of representatives developed a direction of its own, one that extended beyond the United States. With markets opening up in Canada and Puerto Rico, we were doing "international" business. It was international credit repair, rather than "national." In 1999, the year I cut my hair, we changed our name to ICR Services. Inc.,

We created an attractive program for our representatives called "Window Talk."

Designed to attract new prospects, particularly small businesses, the program offered free credit repair services to those who would be willing to display decals representing our various services — a $400 value at the time.

The program allowed our representatives to advertise their ICR business while giving participating businesses an interest-peaking advertisement to draw traffic into their stores.

Astonishing milestones kept coming. By 2000, we reached a five-year growth rate of 73,000 percent. In 2001, *Inc Magazine* named us the 28th fastest growing private company in America.

We had turned down an offer of $10 million from a company that I believe would have shelved my credit repair program and denied consumers the opportunity to exercise their rights. The gamble not only produced unfathomable rewards for the co-founders of ICR Services Inc., but financial freedom for our customers and lucrative careers for thousands of our independent representatives.

My lifelong dream was to start a company where my family could work and share in its success. Little did I imagine that I would also receive a new family, one that extends beyond blood lines and is bonded by a common vision of people working together to turn their lives around.

My journey is not unlike the stories of our customers and our reps. That is the greatest blessing of all of this. We're in the business of new beginnings, and it's contagious.

Charles Safie, the uncle who taught me about the marketing side of business as a child, had a favorite expression he used to quote when he wished people well. We use it today on the folders for our customer service packets:

"May the most you wish for be the least you get."

My Uncle Charlie is a very wise man.

CHAPTER 19

FAITH AND PROMISES

With our sales force up and running, I devoted my energies to the corporate side of ICR Services for the new millennium. But the entire journey also has allowed me to discover and develop a quality of life that goes well beyond the corporate bottom line.

I developed a "center" — a faith.

The religion or the denomination is not important. What I've discovered is common in all the great spiritual paths. It is a faith requiring *action* as well as belief. In fact, I would say that without the manifestation of action, there is no faith. As Saint Paul wrote, "Faith without works is dead." For me that translates into a method as well as a statement. If you want to increase your faith, take action for the good and faith will be given to you.

I am secure in my faith. Although my understanding of God's specific purposes from day to day may lack precision, I believe that it is His will that we all love each other, and help each other as much as we can.

I have believed this since boyhood. However, years ago it often seemed that the only way I could help someone was by confronting bullies. Helping a person often meant giving someone a "physical lesson." That way of "helping" other people has faded away. Someday we — as individuals, splinter groups, and nations — will have to learn to live together on our crowded sphere without using force. It won't happen soon. Maybe no one alive today will live to see it, but universal peace may come to the world in God's good time.

I've always believed the key to my personal growth is to surround myself with people who have qualities that help me be a visionary. Years ago, I remember sitting in class, knowing I wanted to have a company that would be one of the most powerful corporations in the world. My excuse for not working hard in school was that most of what was presented wouldn't help me achieve my goal. I knew instinctively what was important, at least, to me.

My teachers would ask me why I wasn't applying myself in certain subjects. I'd answer their question with one of my own: "How is this going to help me build a company?" I'd tell them, "When I have my company, I'll hire someone to do that, and I'll do what I do best: I'll oversee the business."

But now I realize there is something much more personally rewarding to be attained in any endeavor, whether pursuing an education, building a company or working on personal growth. That's where the *action* part of faith comes in.

I've seen the principle at work with our old family friend Jerry O'Conner. In his early thirties, Jerry was an alcoholic, and his life was on the skids. Now he has more than 40 years of sobriety. He also remains one of our leading reps. He has accomplished his sobriety and rewarding life not only by refusing to drink, but by helping others stay sober in Alcoholics Anonymous. In other words, Jerry has found that in helping others, he also helps himself.

"You have to give it away to keep it," Jerry said.

For me, it translates this way: You want to grow? Help others to grow. You want to succeed? Help others achieve success. You want more vision, help others attain their vision. You want love? Then give love, fully and unconditionally.

For by love's most noble definition, that's what love demands.

Meeting my cousin Enzo provided such blessings. It happened on a business trip Abood and I made to New Jersey and New York. While there, I looked up my cousin Gina. We made dinner plans for later in the week. She said she wanted me to meet her brother.

"His name is Richie," she said. "But everyone calls him Enzo."

I was waiting for Gina to get ready for our dinner engagement when the door opened to her house. I watched as the young man clomped inside. He looked disheveled. His hair was bleached. A metal ring pierced his tongue.

I thought, no way is this Gina's brother. This is some neighborhood punk.

He plopped down, then slumped at the dining room table where I was sitting.

"So, you like my sister?" he asked almost defiantly. He thought I was a date.

"I love your sister," I said.

"You love my sister?" He sounded alarmed. "And who are you?"

"Bernadino Pavoné. And who are you?"

"Richie Pavone," he said, making the last syllable rhyme with "phone."

"You should learn how to pronounce your last name," I said. "It's Pavoné. And I'm your cousin."

His eyes lit up and he sat straighter in his chair. "You're my cousin? How come I never heard about you before?"

"How come I never heard about *you* before?" I shot back.

I already knew some of his background. He'd been addicted to drugs. He'd done everything. He cleaned up on his own and survived. Two of his best friends didn't. A car hit one, probably when he was high, and the other was shot. His dead friends' initials are tattooed on Enzo's shoulders.

When we went to dinner, Enzo spent a lot of time telling me how great a dancer he was. I thought, this kid can't stop bragging about his dancing, so he must not be that great. As a rule, people who know it don't have to tell it. So we found a club with a dance floor and I put him on the spot.

He was unbelievable. The crowd circled him. They clapped and yelled. He stole the evening.

The next day, Enzo and I had a soda together. I looked in his eyes and saw myself all over again. He was a young guy who just turned 21, and I knew right where he was headed. He was living in the worst part of town. But I was in the position to take some action. I was in the position to give some of my success away.

"I want you to come visit me for a week," I said.

He hemmed and hawed.

"It's done," I said. "You're coming."

He finally agreed.

When he arrived in the Detroit area, my mother wanted to kill me.

"This is not a freak show," she said. "What are you bringing in here?"

She turned to Enzo and ordered him to take the tongue ring out and fix his hair. No one will ever be able to accuse my mother of being indirect.

But Enzo listened. He did what he was told.

His stay was a productive one. I told him the story of our company. I took him to ICR and gave him work to do. We went to the gym, dinner and a few nightclubs. I introduced him to my friends. I wanted him to see the good life that came with focus and effort.

I wanted to give him the vision.

After Enzo went home, I told my mother and Abood that I wanted Enzo to move here permanently. I believed he had star potential. My mother thought I was setting myself up.

"I don't want you to get your heart broken if it doesn't work out," she said.

I said I have to take this a chance. I'm committed to it.

Enzo has been with me ever since. He started by filing paperwork with our company. He doesn't do that anymore. Learning the business very quickly, he was promoted to Executive Director of Operations.

Enzo has often said that if it weren't for my intervention, he'd be dead. We had long talks about how he could learn from my mistakes. We spent hours dissecting how the lessons of our shortcomings can be transformed into our greatest strengths.

Everyone is worth a new life. We can agree that it's better not to make serious mistakes in life. But we've all said or done things we wish we hadn't, or failed to do certain things we should have done. If we are extremely lucky — like Enzo was, like I was — we pull back, or get pulled back, before we make that final, fatal error.

Any one of us can make mistakes. What makes a mistake tragic is not the mistake itself, but denying it and trying to shift the blame to someone. If we evade responsibility, we also miss the lesson. Making mistakes is a part of life; often it's the only way we learn. We must acknowledge our part without making excuses. That's an easy thing to say, but very tough to do.

It's hard work, but it is work worth doing. Because out of the work will come a faith — a faith that we *can* turn our lives around.

I have many relatives and friends working for ICR Services. I have them here for sound business reasons. I also have them here because I am living a childhood dream. The soul of the old Safie Pickle Company lives on not only in the corporate office suites, but in the network of thousands of our representatives who've brought family and friends into our collective vision. There are exciting opportunities here for anyone with energy, intelligence, and ambition.

I wanted to keep my promises.

Through the years I made a lot of comments to those who were in my life:

"Let's work together."

"It would be great if we could work together some day."

"When I have a successful company, you'll be the first one I call."

James Croteau, an old high school friend, is one of those who heard me make such promises. I remember how the promise began in my senior year. James was in my house, standing at the kitchen table, and I was making predictions.

"I'm going to build a big company one day," I told him. "And when I do, I'm going to call you, James, no matter where the hell you might be."

"Call me for what?" he asked.

"I will ask you to come to work with me."

He laughed. "Okay, Bernadino," he said. "Anything you say."

In 2000, I learned from my mother that my friend was working with a furniture company. I invited him to lunch and we met at a local restaurant.

"Do you remember the promise I made you?" I asked.

He smiled. "I remember, Bernadino. You were a real motivator, even back then."

"Good," I said. "So you won't be surprised that I'm offering you a career."

He almost dropped his food. "Doing what?"

"I don't know," I said. "What do you do?"

James became our manager of design and graphics. Not only is it working out for him financially, he's also doing creative things for us that I never knew were possible in graphic design.

Other relatives and friends joined us at my request. My sister, Theresa, has always been supportive. I brought her aboard as ICR's Vice President of Representative Relations. My cousin, Victoria Safie Cusumano, became our Director of Regional and Advanced Business Training. I've known Chic, as the cousins call her, since she was born. Charles Rashid, Vice President of Business Development and Technical Research and Development, is another of my first cousins. Another cousin, John Faass, works in representative support. My father-in-law, Ron Amatangelo, is Director of Distribution Service; and a brother-in-law, Nick Amatangelo, is vice president of Finance. Randy Orth, our Chief Operating Officer, went to high school with me. Jim Bates, one of my karate instructors, became the Director of ICR's Anti-Fraud Unit. Connie Ballard, wife of Master Rick Ballard, works in the Processing Department. After he was released from prison, my old cellmate, Sergio Aguero, moved back to Venezuela. He does Spanish translations for ICR

Services. I'm still working on my cousin and entrepreneurial soul mate, Stevie Safie, to join us.

I've named only a few. All have unique talents. All work to meet my often demanding challenges. I did not bring them aboard to give them featherbed jobs. I would not insult their individual abilities with patronage.

There were other promises to keep besides jobs.

Theresa Safie Madoun didn't remember the promise I made her when I was 12. She was the cousin along with her sisters, Mary and Renee, who took my sister and me to breakfast and then to school during my parents' divorce.

But I remembered. In the summer of 2001, I walked into a Jaguar dealership and wrote a check. I called her and told her to meet me.

She showed up wondering why I'd ask her to show up.

"Remember," I said. "I promised you a Jag."

She freaked. She said she couldn't possibly accept it.

"Too late," I said. "I've already paid for it."

I did it for me. I didn't do it for her. The gift is for her, but the true reward was for me. I'm the one being rewarded. The car is only a material thing. More importantly, it allowed me to keep my word.

You've got to give it away to keep it.

During one of our trips to the West Coast, I posed a question to Abood. "How can I ever thank you for all the things you've done for me?"

"You don't need to thank me, Bernie," he said. "It goes without saying."

I did anyway. I knew he'd always wanted a Ferrari and I bought him a red Testarosa.

I bought my mother a beautiful home and a Rolls Royce. It was my way of keeping promises I had made to her, promises I concluded, during my depression in the basement of the family home, I would never be able to keep.

We don't just give to people we know. Contributions from the cofounders to charities are in the six figures annually. We support churches, schools, medical research and organizations that tackle social problems.

I want to spread those same messages to our representatives and employees — be gracious, remember your promises.

These principles figure in how we measure financial success at ICR. When people qualify as a sales rep, our Customer Acquisition Bonus rate is nearly double what it is in most companies. We also give new representatives a generous 45 days to qualify to become eligible to receive the CABs. That's 15 more days than most network marketing companies.

I know the mindset of many of our new reps when they join our company. They're looking for a change in life. They're not happy with their jobs. They're not happy with their careers. They're not making enough money. Some are deep in debt. Some have developed bad work habits.

I want to give them the opportunity to make a living that far surpasses anything they could ever dream of in their lives. I want them to *feel* that, because it's one hell of a high. I get very emotional and involved with them because I want them to do it the right way. I've taken what I've learned and put it into a successful training system. I see how confused and scared some are. I can see it a mile away if they're going to fail. Don't do it that way, I say. Please, do it the ICR way.

Our company is all about the practice of working together

toward a common vision which is to be able to take care of your loved ones. But there is one obligation that all of us can embrace with our hearts and minds — and that is caring for one another.

CHAPTER 20

LISA, A LOVE STORY

When we put our own house in order, when we care for others, when we focus on how much love we give rather than how much we can receive, love comes looking for us. I can only speak from experience, because that's the way it happened for me.

My mother always said, "Bernie, find a woman who is smarter than you."

For years, I wasn't sure what she meant by that, but I finally understood. Both partners have to have their own lives — their own self worth, their own independent pursuits. We have to give the other person the dignity to follow his or her own path. If there's something we cannot accept about the other person, can we really change the person? We can only change ourselves. If we're unwilling to accept people for what they are, then we must, for everyone's mental health, have the courage to move on without resentment or revenge. Some couples create a lot of misery for themselves by failing to learn this simple lesson.

Our customers' files are full of sad stories in which divorcing couples have ruined one another's credit as a last attempt to impact each other's lives long after divorces were final.

A short time after my release from prison, I dated a woman for nearly three years. In time, it became clear that my girlfriend's definition of a good relationship differed from mine. We weren't getting along.

On a chilly Thursday night in February of 1999, I headed out to dinner with Enzo, and my sister's boyfriend, Tony Borrello, whom she later married. I was not in a very upbeat mood. I knew I was going to have to end the relationship with my girlfriend in the coming days. I was explaining to Enzo how difficult that was going to be.

Quite by accident, I looked up to see a tall young woman with raven hair walk by. Our eyes met briefly.

I turned to Enzo. "Now that is the kind of woman I'd like to be with," I said. "Isn't she gorgeous? I wonder who she is."

"Bernie, she was looking at me," Enzo said.

"And you're crazy, Enzo," I said.

We spent a couple of minutes jokingly debating the point. Since I hadn't formally ended my existing relationship, I didn't seek out the mystery woman, even to prove Enzo wrong.

However, I talked about her later that week. Something about the way she walked, the way she looked at me, had kindled my imagination. She seemed so sure of herself. I told my sister how she'd caught my eye.

Exactly a week later, Enzo dropped by my house early in the evening. He found me lying on my bed. He knew I was worn out because by then my troubled romance had finally ended.

"What are you doing?" he asked.

"I'm tired. I just want to watch TV and get some rest."

"You know what, Cuz? I don't ask you for too much, but you said we were going out tonight."

"I said that?"

"Yeah, and I'm holding you to your promise. Remember, I don't have any friends here."

Later, Enzo admitted he was applying guilt just to get me out of the house.

We met Theresa and Tony, and for some reason, we decided to go to the same restaurant we'd chosen the previous Thursday. The hostess seated us at a table. I settled in my chair and looked around.

I couldn't believe my eyes.

I nudged my sister. "Theresa, the girl I've been telling you about is sitting over there with all those guys."

Theresa stood up, turned around, and said, "Oh, my God, she *is* gorgeous."

I got excited. "I'm sending her a drink."

Theresa shook her head. "Send her a drink? Come on, Bernie. That's so tacky."

"But she's got all those men around her," I said. "I don't know if she's got a boyfriend, or what. I can't just walk over. I have to send a drink. It's the only way."

Theresa laughed. "Tacky, tacky, tacky."

I sent the drink and about a half-hour later, I made my way over to the bar and lingered for a few minutes. I was delighted when she left her entourage and approached me. Up close, she was even more beautiful. She had flawless skin, soft features and kind eyes.

We talked a bit and she introduced herself as "Lisa Amatangelo."

"Italian. Are you also part Asian?'

"Korean," she responded. "My father is Italian."

I asked Lisa if she could sit down and talk. "Is that group over there your entourage?"

She laughed. "They're friends from school."

She was in her first year at medical school at Wayne State University. *"Find a woman smarter than you."* I could practically here my mother whispering the words in my ear.

Lisa's grandfather's name was Otto Amatangelo. That named sounded familiar and I suspected my family might know him.

"Can you have lunch with me tomorrow?" I eventually asked.

"I have the afternoon free," she said. "I think we could work something out."

I turned to her girlfriend who had joined us, and asked her to come as well.

"That's so nice of you to ask my friend," Lisa said.

"Let's go to lunch. It's done. You're coming."

She agreed to meet me at my office. Lisa was going to be in the neighborhood, and I wanted to introduce her to my mother.

That night, Lisa and I talked until the restaurant closed.

I went home to my mother's house. Enzo was staying over. He headed straight for his room upstairs, and was asleep in minutes. I headed to my room downstairs, but I couldn't settle down. After a little while I quit trying and went up to Enzo's room.

"Enzo, wake up, wake up."

I bounced on his bed and sang, "Amatangelo, Amatangelo."

Bleary-eyed, Enzo sat up and half stared at me. "Get out of here, Bernie. Cuz, let me sleep."

I shook him. "Enzo, do you know what Amatangelo means?"

He mumbled, "It means it's late; it means it's time to sleep; it means..."

"What kind of an Italian are you, Enzo?" I asked. "Amatangelo means *'love of angels.'*"

Enzo yelled, "For the love of God, will you please, please, let me get some sleep?"

My mother heard us shouting and came in the room, asking, "What the hell is going on?"

"Mom, I'm in love," I said. "Tonight, I met the girl I'm going to marry."

She rolled her eyes. "Shut up and get to sleep," she said. "I don't want to hear about any more women!"

"Mom, you don't understand. She's a medical student."

"Oh, great. Another doctor."

"No, remember? You told me to marry someone smarter than me. You'll meet her tomorrow."

I started singing her name again.

We all ended up in the kitchen, the two of them patiently listening to me rave about Lisa. Talking was going to be the only way I'd settle down. We talked until 3:30 a.m.

The first thing in the morning, I called my Uncle George, my godfather. "Do you know who Otto Amatangelo is?" I asked.

"I've known Otto for almost 50 years. He owns golf courses. He's a developer."

"What about the family?"

"Otto is an honorable man. Why do you ask?"

"Uncle George, I met his granddaughter. She's amazing. I'm having lunch with her today."

Before our conversation ended, I received a godfather's lecture. "Now you listen to me very carefully, Bernie. They are a fine family. I want you to treat her with respect."

I couldn't wait for lunch.

But a couple hours later, my heart sank. Lisa didn't show up at the appointed time. Ten minutes pasted, then 15. My mother, working in the office just across from me, couldn't wait any longer. She had a luncheon meeting and had to leave.

I worried. Lisa Amatangelo appeared to have too much character to stand me up without a call, I told myself. I called her apartment. No answer.

Several minutes later, Lisa showed up. She looked tired and drawn.

"Are you okay?" I asked.

"I'm sorry I'm late," she said. "I found out this morning that my grandfather passed away last night."

I was stunned. She'd lost a family member and still had the fortitude to show up for a lunch.

"What are you doing here?" I asked. "I'm so sorry."

"You know what? I asked my dad the same thing. 'Should I go to this lunch, or not?'"

"He told you to come?"

"I told him I was going to call and tell you that I needed to be with my family, but Dad said I should come here and have lunch with you because that's what my grandfather would want."

I looked into her eyes.

She touched my arm. "So let's have lunch," she said.

The lunch lasted two hours. It was probably a welcome diversion from the heavy emotion she and her family no doubt dealt with that morning. We talked about family and the experiences that mattered to us in life. Lisa kept telling me that I reminded her of her uncle — that I could pass for his brother. I called my mother on her cellphone and asked her to join us. She stopped by for coffee and they became instant friends.

"She's a nice girl," my mother told me afterwards. "Just take it easy with her, OK?"

That wasn't easy to do.

I decided the honorable thing to do would be to pay my respects to her grandfather. I also had learned that Lisa's birthday was on February 15, only a couple of days away. I was going to be out of town that day. I wanted to give her a birthday present beforehand.

I decided I could do both in one visit. We'd just met, but when you're infatuated, you do crazy things. I drove to the funeral home, walked into the chapel and went straight to the deceased. I kneeled and said a prayer.

When I got up, Lisa approached, a little shocked to see me. I hadn't told her I was coming.

"I hope you don't mind, but I just wanted to see if you're okay," I explained. "I also brought you a little something for your birthday. I hope it cheers you up."

We talked for a few minutes. Then she said, "I want you to meet my father. Maybe it's not the best time, but I know he'd like to meet you."

I wasn't planning on that. That prospect made me very nervous. I told her I didn't want to interrupt such a solemn occasion. "I'm just going to sit over here on the side," I said.

We sat together. A big family picture was hanging on the opposite wall, put there to honor her grandfather's legacy during the visitation. Lisa told me the photo included all her aunts, and uncles and cousins. I zeroed in on a man in the picture. He resembled me. I looked more closely.

"Hey, that's Alex Pantangelo," I said.

"No," Lisa said. "That's my uncle Alex Amatangelo. That's the uncle I've been telling you about, the one who's so much like you."

I couldn't swallow. I'd known the guy in the photo for 15 years as *Pantangelo*. He knew my cousins. When we'd see him in bars it would be, "Hey, Pantangelo, what's up?" We called him Pantangelo because it was one of the character's names in the "The Godfather." It was a joke. Probably somebody knew his real name and started it, but the rest of us never knew he was an Amatangelo.

I couldn't swallow because Alex knew my entire story. He knew I'd been to prison. My heart was pounding. Alex was going to tell Lisa my past, and it was all going to be over just like that.

I could hardly breathe as she began introducing me to her family. And then, suddenly, there was Alex. I froze as he came up and hugged me.

"Thanks so much for coming," Alex said. "I really appreciate your coming. Who told you?"

I said, "Alex, I'm very sorry about your father, but I'm really here for your niece."

"Which niece?"

Lisa was distracted, talking to someone else.

"Lisa."

"How do you know Lisa?" Alex asked.

"I took her to lunch the other day."

Alex smiled. "That's cool," he said, nodding. "That's all right."

I caught my breath. Seconds later, she took me over to her father. He was a distinguished-looking man with salt and pepper hair. I was uncomfortable at first, but when he talked, I fell in love with the man. He was very warm and made me feel welcome.

I told myself he'd make a great father-in-law.

I know it all sounds crazy, but that's what I was thinking. It was as if I was powerless to stop the fast-moving chain of events that had brought us together. And I didn't want to stop it. That's the way it was for both Lisa and me. Later, she would tell me she felt attracted to me when she first saw me at the restaurant.

We saw each other every day after the funeral. I told her about my life, about prison. She was willing to get to know me as I was, rather than focus on what I had been.

Our whirlwind courtship, however, was about to face a major time out. Before the funeral, she'd scheduled a vacation with girlfriends to Acapulco. I drove her to the airport and hid a note in her luggage, saying how much I would miss her.

I hadn't anticipated how much.

Hours after I dropped Lisa off at the airport, I called my mother. "Mom, this isn't normal," I said. "There's got to be something wrong with me. I miss this girl so much, it hurts."

She tried to shock me back to reality. "Get over it. You just slow down, and get your butt back to work!"

Later that night, Lisa called me to tell me she arrived safely. It was the beginning of a series of daily phone calls. We called each other a lot.

A day or two later, I was in a hardware store getting some things for the house when my cellphone rang. It was Lisa. I ran outside, the phone pressed to my ear. I told her my feelings. I couldn't hold them in anymore.

"I know I've just met you and it's crazy, but I really miss you."

"I really miss you too," she said.

Apparently her girlfriends surrounded her, trying to listen in to find out what's going on in her life. I was having a hard time getting my thoughts out.

Lisa asked, "What's wrong?"

I could hardly speak.

"Just tell me," she said.

"I want you to know that meeting you has been the best thing that's happened in my life," I said. "Te amo mucho. In Spanish that means 'I love you very much.'" Why not? She was in Mexico.

"What?"

The phone started breaking up.

"Can you hear me?" I asked. "I said, I've fallen in love with you."

"You have?"

I said, "Don't say anything. I just want you to know that. I've got to go. Be safe. I love you."

We'd known each other not even two weeks.

Later, she told me that I'd ruined her vacation. She couldn't fully enjoy her friends or the beach or the scenery. She couldn't wait to get back, she said.

When she returned, I had to leave on a cruise with several family members. I could only call her from a stateroom phone. The calls were $10 a minute. I accumulated a $2,000 phone bill that week, but she was worth every penny.

When I returned we saw each other almost every night. She came to work at the company during the summer break from medical school, helping on several projects.

And on it went… .

Four months after I met her, I invited Lisa and her family to our

ICR Services national convention, held that year at the Novi Hilton, northwest of Detroit.

Three hundred people packed the banquet room. They were ICR reps — my extended ICR family. At the end of the program, my mother, Abood and others took the stage to make some award presentations to representatives and employees.

Near the end of the program, Abood and I presented Mom with a crystal vase inscribed to the "Woman of the Century". She accepted it and said a few words to the audience which applauded warmly.

I turned and reached for another crystal vase and presented it to Lisa. At first, she appeared to think it was for helping us at the company during the summer.

A second later, I saw her eyes focus on the glass and the inscription:

"Lisa, I love you. I adore you. Will you marry me?"

She cried and was shaking, almost dropping the vase.

Soon there were plenty of tears in the audience as well. I knelt on one knee and proposed in front of the crowd.

She extended her hand. I slipped on the engagement ring.

We were married on May 18, 2002, a month before her graduation from medical school.

CHAPTER 21

THE ROAD TO VILLA FLORE

"Do it now!" "It's done!" "I'll see you at the top!" These are some of my favorite phrases. They find their way into our company literature and my presentations at ICR Services conventions.

They're more than marketing slogans; they're an effective way of life. Nowhere was that more aptly demonstrated than the purchase of Villa Flore, the Sacramento, California estate the co-founders purchased in 2001.

The opportunity presented itself quite unexpectedly in the fall of 2000, following a judicial conference attended by Wade McCree, my former attorney in the nightclub development years. Wade's legal career had taken a prestigious turn since the 1980s when he introduced me to the Fair Credit Reporting Act. In 1996, Michigan Governor John Engler appointed him to the 36th District Court in Detroit. At the Stanford Law Alumni Association conference, Judge McCree, a Stanford law graduate, was honored by Willie L. Brown, Jr., the mayor of San Francisco. The mayor proclaimed October 26 "Judge Wade McCree Day" and gave him the key to the city.

Abood and I attended the ceremony with California ICR reps Harmik Poghossian and Bob Hansen, who knew the mayor. Harmik is a great story in his own right. A 20-year-veteran real estate professional, Harmik had joined ICR Services in its formative years, at first considering it as a venture to explore "on the side." As he put it, "I was skeptical at first. It sounded a little too good to be true. But what I've experienced has been the equivalent of flying a Cessna airplane only to find out you're suddenly strapped into the space shuttle rocketing to the moon!"

Harmik, with thousands of reps in his sales organization, became the first independent representative to be named Corporate Executive which is the highest position in the company structure for our sales representatives.

After the McCree presentation, Harmik and Bob wanted to take Abood and me out to dinner. As we drove off in Bob's car, he talked about the kind of quality work he did in a landscaping business he owned. For a little show-and-tell, he casually handed me a color picture of a beautiful estate.

I did a double take. "Hey, I want this," I said.

"Keep it," Bob said. "I've got plenty of them."

No, I want *the estate*."

"What?"

"I want to buy this!"

Bob started laughing. "It was seven million, reduced to three-and-a-half million, Bernie. That's a lot of money, not to mention a lot of upkeep. It's a pretty impressive place."

Villa Flore sat atop the highest hill in a gated community called Los Lagos. The estate was composed of three residences in all: an 8,000-square-foot mansion, a 3,200-square-foot guesthouse, and a 2,300-square-foot pool house. Its original owner had passed away.

At $3.5 million, the price seemed a bargain in California's high-priced real estate market.

Abood, sitting in the back seat, reached for the picture.

"That *is* beautiful," he said.

"Do you have a realtor?" Bob asked.

Harmik piped up in the back seat. "Hey, I'm a broker!"

I said, "It's done, we have our broker."

I kept the picture. On the long flight back to Michigan, Abood and I talked about the estate. There was a way we could make Villa Flore part of the ICR visions, we decided. But we anticipated a problem. We didn't think my mother would go for the proposal.

"The first thing Mom will do is throw the shoe and say, 'no,'" I told Abood. "She'll freak out, but afterwards, she'll calm down. I want that estate."

We gave the presentation to my mother on our return. "Mom, I want this," I said. "But I want you to go see it first."

I handed her the photo.

She stared at the picture for a few moments, looked up and said, "Oh, my God, I want to see this."

Abood and I looked at each other, a little stunned. "Are you serious?" I asked.

She not only was serious, she was already working out the visit. She had a wedding to attend in Las Vegas the coming weekend. "I'll fly to Sacramento from there," she said.

Harmik picked my mother up at the Sacramento Airport. Since he lived in Southern California, which was several hours away by car, he only had time for a quick inspection of the house before my mother arrived.

We later laughed at what he told her in the car. "The main house is huge," he said. "But it has a very small living room."

He was mistaken. As they toured the home, it became evident that the "small living room" was actually a waiting room for guests. The living room is impressively large. The house's many windows and high ceilings flooded the interior with light. The guesthouse was accented in acrylic, including a lavish acrylic staircase imported from France and a $27,000 acrylic table. There was a $37,000 white leather wraparound sofa. Other amenities included a theater room, tennis court, swimming pool with spa, two wine cellars, two garages (one for nine cars), and access to Lake Folsum behind the Estate.

My mother called me after the tour. "You've got to see this," she said. "I want it."

I toured Villa Flore two weeks after my mother. Mom, Lisa and I flew to Sacramento, and then flew to the estate from the airport by helicopter. (The estate has a heliport on one of the houses.)

Simply, Harmik is a great real estate broker. I learned much from watching the way he would drive a hard bargain, but do it with integrity and grace. On our visit, we met the father of the former owner. Harmik and I complimented him frequently on the beauty of the home. Some buyers, in an effort to drive down a price, will often criticize a house, detailing its flaws. That's a self-defeating strategy that destroys many potentially good deals. A home usually is something *personal* to the person who is selling it. Criticizing it can be the emotional equivalent of slamming a member of the family. As a result, sellers will often harden their position out of spite.

During the tour, Harmik described room sizes, furnishings and other details.

I stopped him. "Harmik, I already have a house in Michigan," I said. "This is really not for me. It's for the ICR reps."

He appeared taken aback. "What do you mean?" he asked.

"We're buying this so our top representatives can come to this place and enjoy it," I said. "Not many of them come from this kind of wealthy background, and neither do I. Conferences here will let them see firsthand what their dreams and hard work can bring."

The plan the co-founders had devised was to use the estate to host special conferences for reps who were demonstrating outstanding motivation and leadership. Villa Flore was going to be the location for prestigious company leadership conferences.

"That's the purpose, that's my passion," I told Harmik. "So there's nothing for anyone to sell me. We're buying it, and it's just a matter of negotiating the best price and terms. I trust you for that, Harmik, so do it now!"

After the tour, we began serious negotiations. We negotiated the deal in spite of one company attorney who tried to talk me out of it. He questioned whether the timing was right and the long-term investment potential of large homes geared toward celebrity buyers.

"Other deals will come your way," he said.

"The deal is now," I said.

We closed the sale at $2.8 million, including $400,000 worth of furnishings. It was an exceptionally good price. The estate was valued at various times between $6 million and $8 million around the millennium. Harmik worked very hard putting it all together, but said he wasn't going to accept any commission for being the buyers' agent.

The co-founders argued with him.

"You're going to accept it," I said.

"No, you keep it," he said.

But I wasn't thinking of Harmik. I was thinking of his growing family. "Harmik, you don't understand," I told him. "It's not for you, it's for your new daughter. Do you want to deprive your daughter of her education?"

We finally convinced him to take the substantial commission and closed on January 22, 2001, which was my mother's birthday.

I often talk about the estate in my presentations at our meetings. I grew up in a middle-class family and I am overwhelmed when I stay at the estate. Hard work, focus and the principles we follow at ICR Services made it all happen. I call that journey "the road to Villa Flore." I explain the journey not to brag about the luxuries in my life, but to inspire others to find and follow the road to their dream, whatever that may be.

The co-founders incorporated that vision into one aspect of the design changes at Villa Flore after the purchase. In the guesthouse, which we renamed the Executive House, arriving visitors and representatives walk into an expansive great room where we often entertain. Fixed in the ceiling is a circle with the ICR logo etched in plexiglass and lit by soft shades of neon. Underneath is written another one of my favorite phrases, and it's pretty hard to miss it.

It says, "Global Vision — Let Your Future Begin."

EPILOGUE

OCTOBER 18, 1999

It was a day as significant as the one that took me to Manchester, Kentucky five years earlier. But this car ride would be quite a bit shorter and this trip wouldn't require my mother or my sister to drive.

A brilliant fall morning greeted me when I pulled out of the driveway of my home. Maples and oaks lined the streets and colored yards with splashes of red and gold. I took the freeway for the half-hour drive, catching the last of the Motor City rush hour. The western suburbs gave way to Detroit's struggling neighborhoods. A few miles from downtown Detroit, I saw the gleaming tall towers of the Renaissance Center.

My destination was the Federal Building, the courtroom of U.S. District Judge Nancy G. Edmunds, the judge who'd sent me to prison in 1994. I needed to appear for a motion by my attorney to "terminate supervised release." Even as Abood, my mother and I were building, then operating, ICR Services, I had been on a closely supervised release.

My probation was scheduled to last five years after my release. I had a year and a half left on that. I'd been reporting to my probation officer, Merideth Bratt Boylan, and making payments toward the $93,059 in restitution ordered as part of my prison sentence.

My parole officer knew as much about the conception and growth of ICR as she did my personal life. She often accommodated my busy schedule, but also was very thorough. She had to approve all out-of-state travel, and I was doing quite a bit of that building the company. I also had to meet with her twice a month. We usually met at the Federal Building, but she also came out to my house and my office at times. It was her job to confirm that I was doing what I said I was.

She did her job well.

My attorney, Christopher Andreoff, believed if I could pay off the rest of my restitution and make a request to Judge Edmunds to terminate my probation, she might grant it.

The courtrooms at the old federal building in downtown Detroit are impressive. They are large and adorned with finely crafted wood paneling and matching benches. They are beautiful, in fact. But when my case was called at 10:15 a.m. — "the United States of America versus Bernard Pavoné" — I was hoping I'd never see another federal courtroom again.

I took my seat at the defendant's table and Chris Andreoff addressed the court. Right off, Judge Edmunds wanted to know how much I'd paid toward my restitution.

My attorney said about $15,000 had been paid toward the $93,059. He pointed out that some of the other defendants charged with me had not completed their payments.

"Well, I'm not concerned how much they've paid at this point," Judge Edmunds said. She looked at me and continued, "I'm concerned how much he's paid, and with your suggestion in your papers that he intends to pay the balance somehow, how is he intending to do that?"

Andreoff told her I would pay it with a "bonus distribution" I'd received that year. The judge looked at us curiously. My attorney prepared to hand her some corporate paperwork from ICR Services, but she waved him off.

"I just want to know what job he has," she said.

My attorney tried to explain what I did.

"He is affiliated with a company called ICR Services. They provide… financial services. They provide a service and software to various franchises of — not franchises. That's the wrong word. Sales agents who then interact with other outside people for purposes of avoiding bankruptcy. It's debt reconciliation. He provided — he provides the software; he provides the other services. There's another branch of the company that deals with major corporations which we will be glad to share with the Court under oath."

Andreoff pointed out he'd shared with the U.S. Attorney ICR's financial statements for the last two years, adding "I have his last two years' tax returns as well."

Judge Edmunds put up her hand. "Well, okay, I believe you. So he's got a lot of money coming in. So when does he plan to pay the balance of his restitution?"

"Today," my attorney said.

A couple of moments of silence passed.

The judge turned to the assistant federal prosecutor, asking if she had any objection. She told the Court that the U.S. Attorney's office did not object because my probation officer had also recommended my early termination. However, the assistant prosecutor asked that the judge not sign a termination order until after my check cleared.

The judge nodded. "That's fine with me," she said. "As soon as the check clears, I'll terminate the supervised release. It's an unusually long supervised release period anyway for this, and I think (that was done) because of the amount of restitution that was owing. Ordinarily, even with drug crimes, that sort of thing, you get about a three-year supervised release. He's beyond that period, made regular payments, has no problems that I understand of any kind with his rehabilitation, so as soon as I have some documentation that the check has cleared… I'll sign an order terminating supervised release."

It was almost over.

Before it was, my attorney addressed the judge one more time. "Mr. Pavoné wants to say something to the Court," Andreoff said. "Would he be permitted to do so?"

She looked at me. "Sure."

I stood.

"Thanks, Your Honor," I said.

I'd been curious for years about something I'd done the day I was sentenced.

"In 1994," I said, "I went to your office and talked to your law clerk and asked her to tell you '*thank you*' for what you did. Did you ever get that message?"

"I did."

"And I still say thanks because I'm working hard."

She looked at me for a few moments. "You obviously are," she said.

"I worked hard while I was in prison and I studied real hard. You let me finish my degree, and I graduated from Eastern Michigan… "

I paused. I wanted to savor my next words.

"I've been waiting a long time to tell you this, but your system worked, and I'm not done working... the justice system works if you let it work, and you helped me out, and I just want to tell you, thanks."

She smiled. "Well, I really appreciate you wanting to say that. I'm very impressed with what appears to be an outstanding effort on your part to put this matter right, and I wish you all the best of luck."

"Thank you, Your Honor, very much," I said.

Then she added, "I know you'll be successful."

Later, I thought about what the word "successful" meant to me. I was joining a group of people who've managed to make imprisonment a key turning point in their life. We've all read about some of them:

- Watergate figure Charles Colson created a successful Christian ministry that touched thousands of inmates.
- Michael Milkin, convicted of securities fraud, re-emerged as one of the most sought-after financial advisors in America.
- Tim Allen was incarcerated for drug dealing as a young man and became one of the most beloved comics in the world.

Others are less celebrated. They are ordinary people who simply went home to their families and led good lives. Their accomplishments are no less important than those who make the headlines.

As for me, "success" is a perpetual calling. Some people say I have been successful already. But I don't agree — not yet. When ICR's employees and representatives enjoy financial security — and the freedom that emanates from it — then I will feel successful.

As for the financial restitution, I waited for federal authorities to apply some previous payments and compile a final figure. When the math was done, I wrote a check for $69,754 to the U.S. District Court.

The check, of course, cleared. I knew it would as I drove away from the Federal Building. The money was in my account not only because of my work, but the effort of thousands of people who have come to believe in the vision we call ICR Services, Inc.

I drove back to the office. When I walked through the doors of the company. I felt for the first time like I was a CEO. I told myself, I'm finally on my way.

I kept a photocopy of the check I'd made out to the court. Later, I put the copy with the rest of the materials I'd been saving: the indictment, the assault reports, court records, my prison papers, and even the orientation manual from one of the federal institutions where I'd stayed.

I find myself keeping the justice system paperwork in old Federal Express envelopes. The resilient overnight mail containers make handy storage packages. I started using them to save money in the days when all I could see ahead of me was a mountain of debt. Maybe there's a subconscious reason I still keep the material in those Fed Ex packs. Their contents represent a part of my life that delivered a message of the highest priority.

I keep all of the material in a tiny room under the stairs of my home in Michigan. I want it under the same roof where I eat and sleep. I sleep pretty well knowing *that* part of my life is locked away, and that I have the key to keep it that way.

My life is very full. My bedtime is 1:30 a.m., sometimes 2:00. Every morning, I'm up by six and work out for 90 minutes. On weekends, I work out in the afternoons. I'm very health conscious. I don't eat fats, butter, or oils — no breads, cereal, rice, and very few carbohydrates. I'm on a very high protein, no-fat diet with lots of salads, ground turkey prepared different ways, lots of chicken breasts, fish, and lots of fruit. It's a very energy-laden diet, which I need.

I stay in shape — physically and mentally — and I also have saved other "mementos" from the bad times. I have kept my prison ID cards locked in a room in the executive suite of our corporate headquarters. It's important for me to look at them sometimes. I need to see the photos of my face staring at that prison camera. Sometimes I need to look into those empty eyes, and remember the scared, lonely man I see on the card.

I relish the ability to look other people in the eyes. That wasn't a given in the days I'd lost my way. I meet with dozens of people on any given day. Some are family, friends, and colleagues. Others are new reps who come to our world headquarters for a tour or training or just to check out what we do.

I enjoy meeting new people — every day people. I meet them in airports, restaurants, department stores, service stations and convenience stores. Some appear content, while others look as if they are imprisoned by their lives. I always engage their eyes. I want them to see the hope, joy, and gratitude that fills my heart. I wish I could tell every one of them that if I came back from a self-made disaster, so can they, no matter what their challenges.

There are many perspectives from which we can choose to view our lives. Given the choice between mud and stars — I choose to see the stars — a choice that has made all the difference in my life. I can only hope the others choose to see the stars as well. ■